border to border · teen to teen · border to border · teen to teen · border to border

TEENS IN GHANA

Global
connections

Teens in GHANA

by Myra Weatherly

Content Adviser: David Owusu-Ansah, Ph.D.,
Professor of African Studies, History Department,
James Madison University

Reading Adviser: Alexa L. Sandmann, Ed.D.,
Professor of Literacy,
Kent State University

Compass Point Books ✦ Minneapolis, Minnesota

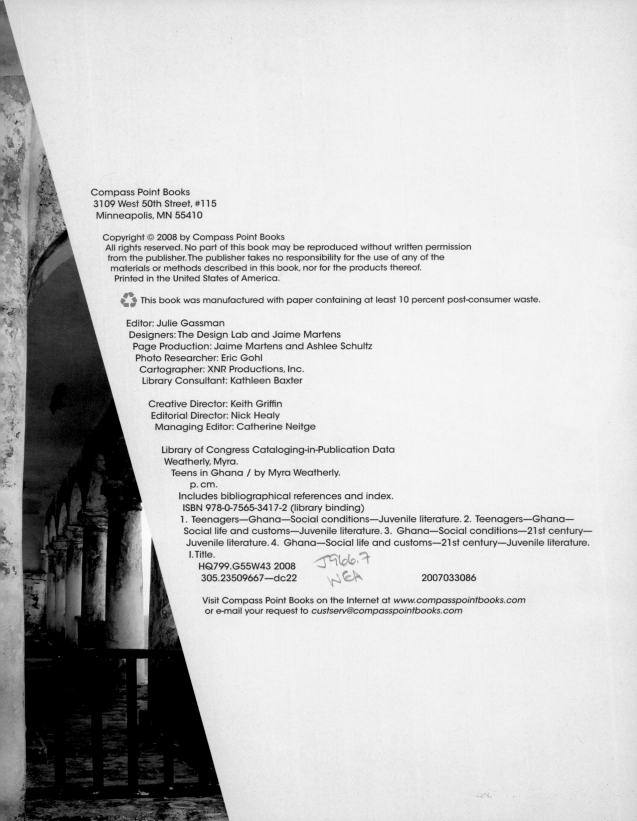

Compass Point Books
3109 West 50th Street, #115
Minneapolis, MN 55410

This book was manufactured with paper containing at least 10 percent post-consumer waste.

Editor: Julie Gassman
Designers: The Design Lab and Jaime Martens
Page Production: Jaime Martens and Ashlee Schultz
Photo Researcher: Eric Gohl
Cartographer: XNR Productions, Inc.
Library Consultant: Kathleen Baxter

Creative Director: Keith Griffin
Editorial Director: Nick Healy
Managing Editor: Catherine Neitge

Library of Congress Cataloging-in-Publication Data
Weatherly, Myra.
  Teens in Ghana / by Myra Weatherly.
    p. cm.
  Includes bibliographical references and index.
  ISBN 978-0-7565-3417-2 (library binding)
  1. Teenagers—Ghana—Social conditions—Juvenile literature. 2. Teenagers—Ghana—
Social life and customs—Juvenile literature. 3. Ghana—Social conditions—21st century—
Juvenile literature. 4. Ghana—Social life and customs—21st century—Juvenile literature.
  I. Title.
  HQ799.G55W43 2008
  305.23509667—dc22   2007033086

J966.7
WEA

Visit Compass Point Books on the Internet at *www.compasspointbooks.com*
or e-mail your request to *custserv@compasspointbooks.com*

Table of Contents

ATLANTIC
OCEAN

Accra ⊛

GHANA MAP

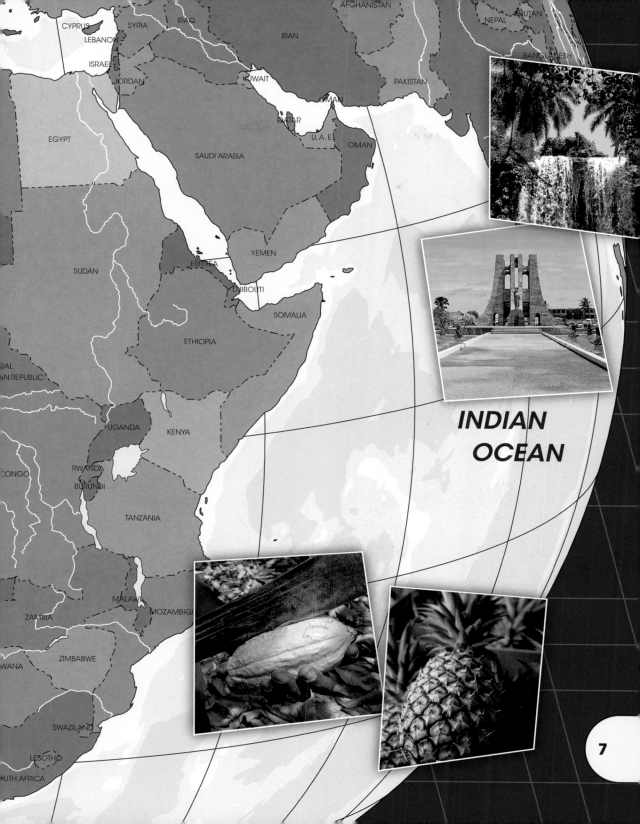

CYPRUS

LEBANON

SYRIA

IRAQ

ISRAEL

JORDAN

KUWAIT

IRAN

AFGHANISTAN

NEPAL

BHUTAN

PAKISTAN

BANGLADESH

EGYPT

SAUDI ARABIA

QATAR

U.A.E.

OMAN

OMAN

SUDAN

YEMEN

ERITREA

DJIBOUTI

SOMALIA

ETHIOPIA

...RAL
...AN REPUBLIC

UGANDA

KENYA

...CONGO

RWANDA

BURUNDI

TANZANIA

MALAWI

ZAMBIA

MOZAMBIQU...

ZIMBABWE

...WANA

SWAZILAND

LESOTHO

...UTH AFRICA

*INDIAN
OCEAN*

TEENS IN GHANA

IN GHANA, LIFE FOR TEENS VARIES SIGNIFICANTLY. There is no one way to explain what it is like in this small west African country. Family as well as religious and tribal practices influence teens. Living environments, too, play a vital role in their lives. Often rural teenagers marry young. They become farmers or cattle herders to feed the family. Some teens work at stone quarries. "After school I work for my uncle at the stone quarry," says Moses. "I cut stones with a chisel and hammer. … When I grow up, I do not want to cut stones … so I must study hard in school." On city streets, some teens peddle newspapers. Some shine shoes. Others hawk items in crowded marketplaces. Teens from the upper-income classes play video games and chat on cell phones.

Ghana is a country with a population of more than 22 million. It is a youthful population, with nearly 40 percent under the age of 15. The nation's hope for the future rests on their shoulders. Educating the youth of Ghana for a productive adulthood is a must.

9

With less than 40 percent of its population attending secondary school, one of Ghana's biggest challenges is keeping young people in school.

CHAPTER ONE

The Way Forward

GHANA WAS ONCE A COLONY OF GREAT BRITAIN. During colonization, it was named the Gold Coast for its abundance of gold. It remains one of the world's top producers of gold. Even so, it is a poor country. As Ghana works to overcome poverty, education is seen as the way out. The highest priority is getting children to go to school and stay in school.

When Ghana obtained freedom from British colonial rule in 1957, education became the main concern of the new nation. At the time, Ghana had a scattering of primary schools, a few secondary schools, and only one university. In contrast, today there are thousands of primary and secondary schools. In addition, students who wish to continue their education after secondary school have many more options. There are now more than 50 tertiary (post-secondary) schools in Ghana.

Every year, Ghana spends between 28 percent and 40 percent of its budget on education. During the past 50 years, Ghana has made important strides in education, but there is more to do. Four

11

Teen Scenes

In the capital city of Accra, a 15-year-old girl prepares for school. A live-in maid serves her a fried-egg sandwich and a cup of tea for breakfast. She tucks her cell phone into a designer book bag and, with a final glance in the mirror, she is off. She goes to school by taxi. The car winds its way through the jammed streets. Scents from the many fruit and vegetable stands fill the morning air. Horns blare. Street peddlers carry goods on their heads and walk between the cars, trying to make a sale. The teen will spend her day in a modern school building, filled with well-trained teachers and the latest technology. She takes her schoolwork seriously and works hard. To fulfill her dream of becoming a doctor, she must excel in school.

In the countryside, a 13-year-old girl rises early to help prepare breakfast. After she eats, it is time to walk to school. Though some villages have a simple building or shed for a school, her community uses the shade of a sprawling palm tree as its classroom. After four hours of school, she returns home to do farmwork. She assists her family with the cassava harvest. She bends over, lifts the lower part of the stems, then yanks the root vegetable out of the ground. Her formal education will soon be over. Her parents cannot afford to send her away to secondary school. In a year or two, she will likely be married. Though the legal age for marriage is 18, it is seldom enforced.

In the city of Kete Krachi, a boy in his midteens prepares to go to work. The sky is still dark over Lake Volta. A chill is in the early morning air. He and his crew of 10- to 12-year-olds jump into a canoe. They paddle out onto the lake. A mile or so out from shore, they pull up a fishing net. The net comes up slowly, inch by inch. The teenager supervises the work, which is dangerous for such young laborers. He is not in the fishing business by choice. His parents leased him to a fisherman when he was the same age as his young crew. He has no schooling and freedom, and he never sees the money he earns. Each December the fisherman pays his parents a small sum. The trivial amount keeps his family from starving. His parents live in a region where two-thirds of the population exists on less than one Ghanaian cedi (U.S.$1) a day.

The lives of teens in Ghana vary, depending on their circumstances. Even so, they share a bond: hard work. Whether they are students, farmers, peddlers, or fishermen, they put in many hours of exhausting work.

out of 10 Ghanaian school-age children do not attend school.

The Education System

Ghana's education system is based on the British school system. The public schools have four levels: preschool, primary, junior secondary, and senior secondary. Students who finish secondary school may go on to attend universities or another form of tertiary education.

Changes in the past decade have been positive. In 2002, preschool education for ages 4 and 5 was added. The course work focuses on developing social skills and stresses creativity. Language, mathematics, environment, health, nutrition, and safety are also taught. Eventually every Ghanaian child will have access to a preschool

Ghanaian Schools

Type	Age	Description	Number of schools nationwide
Preschool	4–5	Focuses on development of social skills	6,300
Primary	6–12	Provides a basic education	12,130
Junior Secondary	13–15	A mix of academic and skills-oriented courses	5,450
Senior Secondary	16–18	Prepares students for higher education or job training	503
Training College	post-secondary school	Provides special training in teaching	21
Technical School	post-secondary school	Focuses on science and technology, emphasizing practical skills for related jobs	18
Polytechnic Institution	post-secondary school	Prepares students for careers in engineering and other math- and science-based fields	9
University	post-secondary school	Offers a wide range of programs, from music to accounting to African studies	5 public, 13 private

education. Public schools are free and open to boys and girls.

Primary school starts at age 6 and ends at age 12. The national program for primary schools includes mathematics, science, and social studies. Other areas of study are cultural studies, life skills, and physical education.

Learning a number of languages is important in primary school. A variety of languages and dialects (local versions) are spoken throughout Ghana. For the first two years, students speak their local dialect, and English is taught as a second language. From third grade on, students are taught in English. They speak, read, and write in English. It isn't as tough as it sounds, though.

A Land of Many Tongues

More than 100 languages and dialects are spoken in Ghana. One of the most common is Twi. It is spoken by the Akan ethnic group, who live in southern Ghana. Within the Akan are smaller groups, who speak various dialects of Twi. All forms of the language are rich in proverbs. These sayings show the wisdom of the Ashanti, one of the Akan groups.

Phrases	Pronunciation	Translation
Wo ho te sen?	woe hoy teh sen	How are you?
Me ho ye	may hoy yay	I am fine.
Me da ase	may dah say	Thank you.
Yoo	yoh	You are welcome.
aane	AH-nay	yes
dabi	DAH-bee	no

Many children enter school knowing some English from their parents. In fact, as in many African countries, English is Ghana's official language.

Some students study a third language, too. A large Muslim population occupies the northern regions of Ghana. Muslim students study Arabic (the language of Islam's holy book, the Qur'an) in addition to English.

Beyond Primary School

Exams are a constant source of stress for students. Students can't move beyond primary school without taking a broad national exam. Students need high scores, and competition is fierce. The exams are a major focus in the curriculum. School officials organize practice tests. Teachers use class time to teach exam-related content. Students put forth great effort to prepare for secondary school entrance exams. If they can afford to, parents send their children to extra classes or hire tutors to coach their children.

Students who pass the exams enter junior secondary school for three years, from ages 13 to 15. This is equivalent to middle school in other countries. In 1987, junior secondary schools began offering technical and vocational training in addition to academic courses. As a result, students who do not attend senior secondary school are better equipped to enter the job market.

After junior secondary school,

On a Mission

All Ghanaian languages existed only in spoken form until Christian (mainly Presbyterian and Methodist) missionaries arrived in Ghana from Europe. In the 19th century, missionaries introduced European-style education to the southern regions of Ghana. Soon mission schools dotted the countryside. In the beginning, the mission schools emphasized primary education. The introduction of secondary schools occurred in the early 1900s. These missionaries learned and transcribed the local languages. The Ashanti, Fante, Ewe, Ga, and Dogbane groups have written forms of their languages today through the efforts of the missionaries. Some schools are still religion-based and operate as private schools.

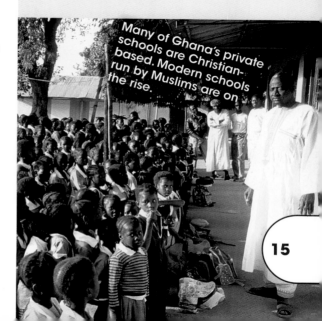

Many of Ghana's private schools are Christian-based. Modern schools run by Muslims are on the rise.

qualified students enter senior secondary school, or high school. Some students attend private boarding schools, which normally charge fees. Because of the added expense, private-school students are mainly from upper-income families. They spend nine months on campus and return home during vacations.

Senior secondary-school students study English, mathematics, science, agriculture, and social studies. They also take a Ghanaian language and physical education. Students may also choose to take courses in special areas, such as business, technology, life skills, and art. They are allowed a maximum of nine courses each semester. Normally, a single class lasts for 45 minutes. Depending on the subject matter, some class periods may last 90 minutes. Teaching methods

During the 1990s, an international program helped bring more computers to classrooms in Ghana. In addition, the government increased funding for computer education.

include lectures, group work, student presentations, and videos. Teachers encourage students to use higher thinking skills.

Generally teenagers take their schoolwork seriously, but they also have fun. They hang out with other teens at school-sponsored sports events, parties, and dances with local and Western music. Football (soccer) is the most popular sport in Ghana. It is played mainly by boys. Both girls and boys play basketball, tennis, and volleyball. Debating is another popular school activity. Topics may include global affairs, political issues, or human rights.

At the end of secondary school, students take another national exam, the West African Secondary Examination. The test requires several days to complete. Test scores determine which university a student will be allowed to attend. They also dictate the courses a student can take. But there are more applicants than the universities can accept. Even those who are accepted by a Ghanaian university often go abroad for higher education, if they can afford it.

Ghanaians like to celebrate. Graduation from secondary school is a big event for students and families. It is a time of speechmaking and awarding of prizes. Family members, decked out in their finest clothes, use digital cameras to record the event.

Netball, similar to basketball, is popular in Ghana school yards.

17

The Future of Education

Ghana's education system has come a long way since independence in 1957. However, increasing challenges of the 21st century demand more progress. Basic education is required for all children between 6 and 15 years of age, but many still do not attend. Poverty and teenage pregnancies account for most school dropouts.

In certain sections of the country, education is not considered essential. In some areas in the northern part of the country, the dropout rate is high. Fewer than 50 percent of students reach the last year of primary school. For boys, work on the family farm replaces schooling. In the case of girls, many parents do not object to early marriage. They have different expectations for their daughters. For example, families whose wealth is measured in cattle may consider a dowry of three cows more important than a girl's education.

In general, more boys stay enrolled in schools than girls. At the primary level, the male-to-female ratio is about one to one. However, the gap widens at the upper levels. In some parts of the country, fewer than 25 percent of females attend secondary school. This reflects traditional social values, which view education for males as more important than for females.

In addition to the dropouts, there are other problems being faced by Ghana's education system. In 2005, the government eliminated school fees, which were used to buy textbooks. The removal of fees meant more people could go to school. The lower educational levels had an increase in enrollment of more than 600,000 pupils. Because of the surging enrollment, schools now struggle with overcrowding. A lack of qualified teachers and

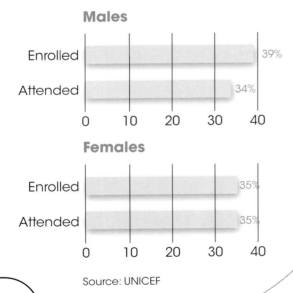

Secondary School Enrollment & Attendance (2000-2005)

Males

Enrolled 39%
Attended 34%

0 10 20 30 40

Females

Enrolled 35%
Attended 35%

0 10 20 30 40

Source: UNICEF

Large shade trees provide an escape from the sun during Ghana's dry seasons. However, there is no protection from rains, and classes are regularly canceled during wet seasons.

poor quality facilities add to the problem. Classes are large, ranging in size from 45 to more than 60 students.

The immediate response to these problems has been to use a shift system. Students attend one of several shifts during the day. Samuel Bannerman-Mensah, director of Ghana Education Service, suggests teaching children outdoors. He asks, "Which is better, a child who doesn't go to school or one who has the chance to be taught under a tree?"

In 2006, Ghana's strained school system received a World Bank grant of U.S.$11 million. This money will be used to build classrooms, buy textbooks, and hire more teachers. Time will tell whether these measures narrow the gap between education for the rich and poor.

Chores, such as collecting water, take up much of the day for many Ghanaians.

CHAPTER TWO

Life in the Gold Coast

WALKING DOWN A GHANAIAN STREET YOU SEE BOYS SHINING SHOES, girls carrying pots on their heads, and people everywhere smiling. Though their backgrounds are diverse, all Ghanaians seem to share a love of life.

But in what ways do Ghanaians differ from one another? Teen boys have different responsibilities than girls. Upper-income families can provide their children with more opportunities than lower-income families can. And different ethnic groups have different customs. Perhaps the biggest factor in defining the lives of Ghanaians is where they live. Ghana is a rural nation, despite a surge in the urban population. In 2005, about 54 percent of the population lived in rural areas. This is a drop from the 1970s, when about 72 percent of the population was rural. The cities are growing rapidly. Each year more people move to the cities seeking better jobs with better pay. Access to electricity and plumbing also lures people to the cities. Teens are moving in greater numbers to Ghana's largest cities, including Accra, Kumasi, and Tamale.

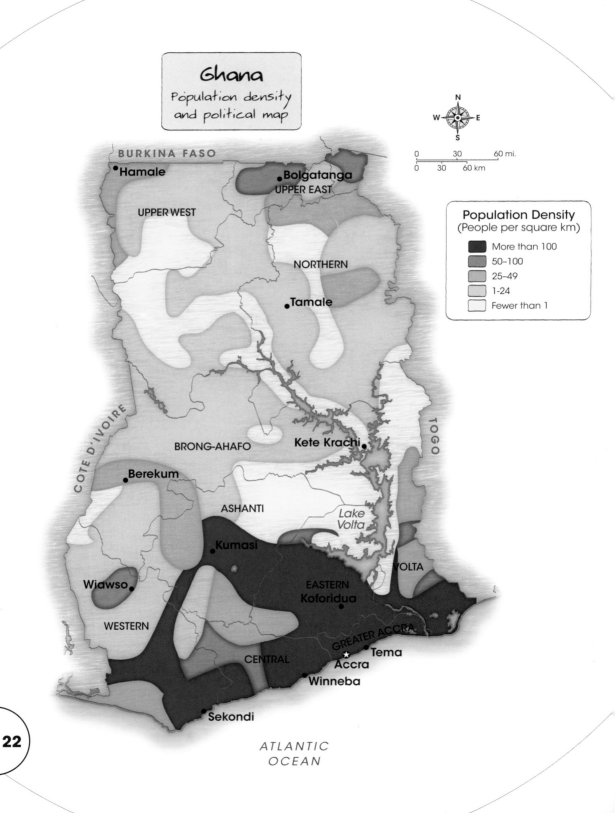

Ghana
Population density and political map

BURKINA FASO

• Hamale

• Bolgatanga
UPPER EAST

UPPER WEST

NORTHERN

• Tamale

COTE D'IVOIRE

BRONG-AHAFO

Kete Krachi •

• Berekum

ASHANTI

Lake Volta

• Kumasi

TOGO

VOLTA

Wiawso •

EASTERN
Koforidua •

WESTERN

GREATER ACCRA
• Tema
★ Accra

CENTRAL

• Winneba

• Sekondi

Population Density
(People per square km)

More than 100
50–100
25–49
1-24
Fewer than 1

N
W E
S

0   30   60 mi.
0   30   60 km

22

ATLANTIC OCEAN

Ghana's Cities

Accra is the largest city in Ghana. It stretches along the Atlantic Coast and north into the interior. When the Portuguese arrived in the late 15th century, the Ga tribes occupied what is now Accra. The area was colonized by the Dutch, English, and Danish in the 17th century. It developed into a prosperous trading center of West Africa. The city of Accra became Ghana's capital in 1877.

Today the sprawling city presents a varied appearance, with its modern, colonial, and traditional architecture. Busy markets line the streets. Not only is Accra the administrative and financial center of Ghana, it is also an important commercial and manufacturing center.

Industries include vehicle and appliance assembly and petroleum refining. Food products, textiles, metal and wood products, plastics, and medicines are all manufactured in Accra. This modern metropolis is also the site of an international airport and the hub of the country's railway system. Its railway and bus systems provide links to other towns, including the nearby port city of Tema. Accra is also the center of cultural activities.

Like most cities, Accra is filled with people from all walks of life. A mix of the rich and the poor lives in Accra. The expanding city has an estimated population of 1.85 million. Those in the upper-income class live in elegant

Though more than 40 percent of residents in the Greater Accra region live in one-room homes, there are also larger modern housing developments.

23

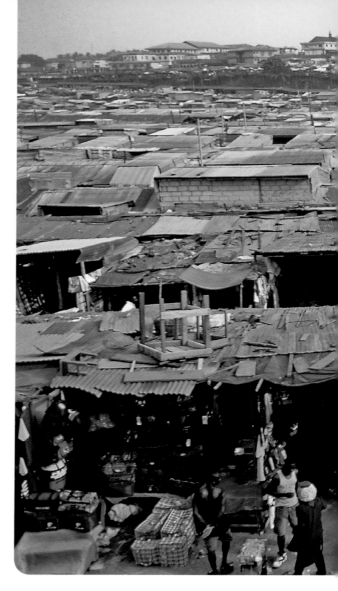

houses filled with modern conveniences. Others own few possessions and live in impoverished areas with poor sanitation.

The second-largest city in Ghana is Kumasi. It is located in the rain forest region of Ghana about 200 miles (320 kilometers) northwest of Accra. Like Accra, Kumasi is an old city. Set on hills and surrounded by forests, the city has a humid climate with high rainfall. It is commonly known as the Garden City because of its lush tropical vegetation. Now a sprawling city, Kumasi is home to an estimated 1.5 million people.

Situated at the junction of main roads, Kumasi is ideal for trade and commerce. Major exports include gold, agricultural products, and high-quality hardwood. Cocoa farming in the area around Kumasi brings in much of the city's wealth. The vibrant central market is one of the largest in western Africa. It serves as a significant source of income for many residents. Shoppers can pick up everything from auto parts to crafts in the market.

In the villages around Kumasi, artisans specialize in crafts such as gold jewelry making, pottery, and wood-carving. Also important is the printing of the traditional *kente* cloth. This cloth is identified by its geometric shapes and multicolored patterns. Bright yellow, orange,

kente
ken-TA

blue, and red are the main colors.

A short walk away from the market is the National Cultural Center, a major attraction. This huge complex houses a museum of history, a popular library, an excellent crafts shop, and

The Kumasi Market, one of the largest markets in Africa, brings in as many as 10,000 traders.

an exhibition hall.

This fast-growing city has a long, rich history. Kumasi was the capital of the Ashanti Kingdom in the 18th and 19th centuries. It continues to serve as the cultural center of the Ashanti people, the largest ethnic group in Ghana. A king reigns over the Ashanti. He receives allegiance from the Ashanti people in Ghana. He is said to be the richest king on Africa's west coast and lives in Manhyia Palace, one of Kumasi's most spectacular buildings.

Very different from both Accra and Kumasi is Tamale, Ghana's third-largest city. Located in the northern region of Ghana, Tamale is flat, and it is dusty most of the year. It is home to more than 350,000 people. It is said that horse-riding invaders from the north founded the kingdom of Dagbon in the 15th century. The kingdom occupied the site of what is now Tamale and the surrounding area. Under British rule, Tamale served as the administrative center of the northern region, a position it still holds.

Tamale is also the busiest commercial center in the north. Produce that is grown in the north is shipped to Tamale. Here it is distributed to other areas of the country. Crops such as cotton, rice, and peanuts are shipped to Accra from Tamale.

Tamale is the principal center of education in the north. It is the site of two government teacher-training colleges and a technical institute. The University of Developmental Studies opened there in 1992. This institution serves the northern part of the country, where poverty is highest. It is part of an effort to bring the standards of education in the north closer to those in the country's southern regions.

Bright Lights, Big City

In all of Ghana's cities, the daily routine of urban teens is similar to that of teens in many major cities worldwide. They wake up early in the morning. They wear a school uniform. After breakfast with the family, they head to school. The school system does not provide transportation, so if the school is near, the teens walk. If not, they may go by taxi or public bus. Parents with cars drive their children to school. The school day usually ends in the middle of the afternoon. Before going home, some students engage in special activities. In addition to school-sponsored activities, teens hang out at the YMCA, participate in environmental clubs, or play sports. Others spend time with friends.

Some teens return home to multilevel mansions. Most of these upper-income homes have whitewashed walls and are surrounded by lush, green gardens. Inside, teens watch television and videos and play computer games. They chat with friends on cell phones— from their own bedrooms. Other city teens live in more modest housing. Often made of brick or concrete, these homes may be single-story or multistory. Though modest, they have modern conveniences, including plumbing.

Urban teens who attend boarding school also rise early. They rush to morning assembly, where prayers are said and announcements are made. Following breakfast, students are in class until lunchtime. Supervised study sessions take place in classrooms or the library. Special activities take place in the evenings. These include sports, movies, and extracurricular activities, such as music, dance, or natural history.

Fashion Corner

Ghanaians, like all west Africans, are style-conscious. Most Ghanaians dress conservatively and consider it important to be properly dressed in public. Shorts are appropriate at the beach but unacceptable in public elsewhere. Western-style dress is standard in most urban areas, especially for young people. Traditional dress is still popular and always worn to ceremonial occasions.

Traditional attire varies by region and ethnic group. Ashanti, Fante, and Ewe men wear robes made of colorful woven strips of kente cloth. In the south, men may wear *ntoma*—colored cloth wrapped around the body somewhat like a toga. The ntoma is often worn over a shirt and shorts. Northern men wear smocks made of wide strips of rough cotton cloth. Muslim men wear robes similar to those worn by Arab Muslims, but the Ghanaian version is more colorful.

For Ghanaian women, traditional dress is a long wraparound skirt, a loose blouse, and a head scarf. They wrap an additional cloth around the hips and often add more cloth to the sleeves. If worn, a head cloth usually matches a woman's dress. Ghanaian women generally prefer bold colors and prints. Gold arm bracelets, hoop earrings, and beautiful glass bead necklaces complement the traditional dress.

ntoma
n-TOH-ma

Leaders, such as President John Kufuor, wear kente cloth robes for important ceremonies.

Throughout the day, boarding schools provide strict supervision for teens.

Teens Who Have Left School

In urban areas, there are also many teenagers who do not attend school. Most have come to the cities to escape poverty. Thousands of these migrants live in shantytowns that skirt the edges of the larger cities. These communities are built in a haphazard manner without defined streets.

Within these shantytowns, many teens live in crowded mud huts with slate or corrugated metal roofs. For others who have become street children, discarded packing cases serve as places to sleep. According to the International Child and Youth Care Network, these teens spend most of their time on the streets trying to make a little money. Because they lack job skills, they may beg, steal, or turn in recycling items for cash. The lucky ones find jobs selling produce in the big city markets.

Unable to find a job in her village, one young girl moved to Accra. She had just completed junior secondary school and was looking for a better life. For two years, she worked as a small trader, selling items independently and paying no taxes to the government. She used her earnings to pay for training to become a hairstylist. Now she works in a small salon in the slum. She hopes to own her own shop one day.

Even if street children are able to find jobs, they face a hard day-to-

Experts see the development of shantytowns as an urban housing problem in Ghana.

day existence. They suffer from hunger, drug use, and physical abuse by other street children, city guards, and police. The government tries to help these young people. In addition, many international organizations have set up programs for them. As a result, many are receiving training in job skills. Their chances of finding a job that pays well are greatly improved.

Villagers carry water back from the village well in a variety of containers.

Mammy Wagons

For many Ghanaians, mammy wagons, a form of public transportation, are a vital part of daily life. The word *mammy* comes from a respectful term used to refer to wealthy women who control trade. They are large trucks with wooden sides. Inside, passengers sit on wooden benches. These rickety vehicles carry passengers and cargo. In the towns, the brightly painted mammy wagons are called *trotros*. They travel around towns and bump along rough dirt roads. Townspeople often travel by mammy wagons to visit relatives in the villages.

trotros
TRO-tros

Rural Life

Rural teens begin their day by rising much earlier than urban teens. Long before sunrise, students begin chores. Boys cut firewood, help on the farm, and fetch water from the village well before walking to the nearby school.

Generally, teenage girls have more responsibilities around the house than boys. For example, a 13-year-old girl in a rural middle school rises early in the morning. She sweeps the house and yard. She helps cook breakfast. She cleans the dishes. Then she feeds her

Animals are allowed to roam the courtyard areas of rural villages.

baby sister. All of this work is finished before school. When she returns home, more housekeeping chores await her. There is little time for homework or fun.

This same teenage girl's rural house is made of earthen walls with a thatched roof of palm leaves. It does not have electricity or indoor plumbing. She sleeps on a simple wooden bed with a mattress and a sheet. She shares a room with her sister. Her two younger brothers share a separate sleeping space, as do her parents. The yard is filled with the noises of barking dogs, clucking chickens, and snorting pigs.

In all likelihood, this 13-year-old—like other rural girls—will become one of Ghana's dropouts before she completes junior secondary school. In a year or two, she may be married. Her husband will likely be a village farm boy who has also dropped out of school.

Food for Thought

Food is one thing that ties nearly all Ghanaians together. Typically Ghanaians eat three one-course meals a day. Breakfast is a hearty meal. A popular dish is *ampesi,* cooked yam, the root vegetable cocoyam, or the bananalike plantain. For lunch, *ken key* is often served. This dish is made from ground white cornmeal soaked in water for two days. Then it is shaped into a ball, which is

ampesi
am-PEH-si

ken key
ken KAY

boiled in water for three to four hours. After boiling, the cornmeal is wrapped in plantain leaves and placed on a rack above boiling water. It steams for a couple of hours before being served with fish or stew.

The most common evening meal is *fufu*. It is a dough mixture, too, made from root vegetables such as cassava, yams, or cocoyam. It is normally served in the shape of a ball. Ghanaians tear small pieces off the ball of dough and roll them into small spheres. Then they dip the small balls into a thick soup of groundnuts (peanuts), fish, beans, or

fufu
FOO-foo

Ghanaians often eat together from one dish, using their right hands rather than utensils.

other vegetables. Another favorite is pepper soup—hot and spicy.

Sweet dishes abound in Ghana—but not as dessert. Ghanaians prefer to snack on sweets between meals. Though Ghana is one of the world's leading producers of cocoa, few sweet dishes include chocolate. Instead, fruit is featured. One popular sweet dish is a pancake made of mashed plantains that have been deep-fried in palm oil. Another sweet snack is made of plantains mixed with corn flour and shaped into balls like doughnuts.

In urban areas, Sunday is often the day for eating out. Restaurants cater to tourists and wealthy Ghanaians. International food is commonly served. Chop bars are cafes that feature local food. They are the Ghanaian version of Western fast food. Street stalls are the cheapest way to eat out. These sell rice with various dishes and fresh fruit.

As in the rest of the world, cola and other sodas are available in Ghana. Made with fresh fruit, Refresh is a soft drink produced in Ghana. Children enjoy its sweet taste. Beer is also popular. *Pito* is another popular alcoholic drink, especially in the northern regions. People living in the south prefer palm wine. There are no laws in Ghana that set a drinking age. However, strong parental control prevents most teenagers from drinking recklessly.

pito
PEE-toh

Western soft drinks, such as Coke, Sprite, and Fanta, are popular refreshments.

Staples & Storage

Ghanaians grow much of their food. This is an easier task in some parts of the country than in others. In areas where weather conditions are extreme, hunger may pose a serious problem for six months of the year. In the north, sometimes a long dry season is followed by a wet season that is too short for growing crops. The climate is less harsh in the south, and the eastern region of Ghana has a mild climate, fertile soil, and abundant rainfall. Large farms in this eastern area produce cash crops that can be shipped to other cities.

Staple foods vary according to region but often include wheat, potatoes, millet, corn, rice, and yams. Cocoyam is a root vegetable that grows wild in the forested areas and is also cultivated. Cassava is another root vegetable that tolerates a wide variety of growing conditions.

In the cities, most people have money and can buy some of their food at markets. The rural areas depend on home gardens, roadside markets, and wild fruit and vegetables for their food supply. Women cook every day. Without electricity, storing food for future use is a problem—with the exception of grains and some dried fruit.

Markets offer fruits and vegetables such as tomatoes and cassava root.

The family is the center of Ghanaian society. Many extended families live and work together.

3

The Family Is a Crowd

A 15-YEAR-OLD GIRL ARRIVES HOME FROM SCHOOL. Upon entering the family compound, she is greeted by a chorus of voices—all her kin. She pauses for a moment in the courtyard and listens as her grandfather spins an old tale. Wide-eyed youngsters sprawl in the sand, hanging onto the storyteller's every word. She remembers how she loved listening to folktales when she was little. Her favorites came from her Ashanti ancestors. Today the children sit spellbound by the story of the spider Anansi (or Asanse), who always gets into trouble. However, in the end, Anansi overcomes all obstacles with his cunning and wise ways.

The family is highly valued by Ghanaians. Two types of families—nuclear and extended—exist in modern Ghana. The nuclear family is a social unit that consists of a father, mother, and their children. For the most part, these are the families who have migrated to the cities, leaving their clan behind. Yet they manage to stay connected to family clans, often traveling long distances to visit and attend festivals.

Many rural Ghanaians belong to extended families. This family unit includes parents and children together with grandparents, aunts, uncles, and cousins—sometimes spanning three or four generations. An ancient Akan proverb states, "The family is a crowd." It is a perfect description of the size of a Ghanaian family.

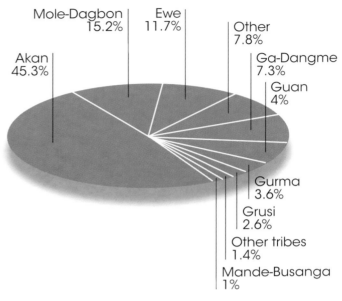

Ethnic Groups in Ghana

Mole-Dagbon 15.2%
Ewe 11.7%
Other 7.8%
Akan 45.3%
Ga-Dangme 7.3%
Guan 4%
Gurma 3.6%
Grusi 2.6%
Other tribes 1.4%
Mande-Busanga 1%

Source: United States Central Intelligence Agency. *The World Factbook—Ghana.*

A Vibrant Ethnic Mosaic

In Ghana, each extended family is descended from a common ancestor. This provides a way to organize families. Ghanaians practice two systems of descent: male and female. In some ethnic groups, members are descended from a common male ancestor. In other ethnic groups, members are descended from a common female ancestor.

Ghana has more than 100 ethnic groups. Each group has its own distinct customs, which affect both daily life and relations within the family. The principal ethnic groups are the Akan, the Mole-Dagbon, the Ewe, and the Ga. The varied beliefs can sometimes lead to cultural tensions. The worst incident occurred in 1994, when 1,000 people were killed in tribal violence. However, this was an extreme situation. In general, Ghanaians from all backgrounds share opportunities in business, politics, and education. They live and work together in peace.

The largest ethnic group in Ghana is the Akan. About 45 percent of the population belongs to this tribe. These people live mainly in the heart of the rain forest. They were the earliest people to have contact with Europeans and Protestant missionaries. Today most are Christians, although they cling to

Kente cloth weavers combine various patterns and colors in their designs. They work with cotton, silk, rayon, or metallic thread.

Words of Wisdom

The Akan people have many proverbs. Some relate to proper behavior. Some offer advice: "If you are in hiding, don't light a fire." Honoring your relatives is reflected in this proverb: "If your elders take care of you while you are cutting your teeth, you must in turn take care of them while they are losing theirs."

traditional religious practices. The tribe traces its ancestry through the mother.

The Akan group includes the Ashanti, the largest single tribe in Ghana. They were once renowned for the splendor and wealth of their rulers. Today they are famous for their craft work. They are admired for their hand-carved stools. Their traditional kente cloth is known worldwide. It is woven on looms by men and boys.

The Mole-Dagbon people make up 15 percent of the population. Living in the northern regions of Ghana, they are the least influenced by modern lifestyles. Most are Muslims. Unlike the Akans, the Mole-Dagbon tribes trace the family line through the father.

Nearly 12 percent of the population belongs to the Ewe tribe. They live in the Volta region along Ghana's eastern border. The Ga tribes inhabit the coastal region around Accra. They make up about 7 percent of Ghana's population.

In all the ethnic groups, the extended family provides the Ghanaian teenager with a strong support system. It instills in teenagers a sense of responsibility to self, family, and community.

The Role of the Family

As in all societies, the family is usually the main source of the basic needs for life and health. Family members help provide housing, food, clothing, and clean water as they are able. In traditional families, the extended family is responsible for the care and upbringing of all children. Within this structure, children occupy a central place. The responsibility for the social development of the child is shared by the members of the community. As a result, the child usually develops a strong sense of responsibility and respect for elders from an early age. The extended family offers a variety of role models to help the young prepare for adulthood.

In families that run shops, the children often stay by their parents' side throughout the workday.

THE FAMILY IS A CROWD

Extended family members live close to each other. Some family members share a residential compound, which is divided into sections. One section is for males only. Women, girls, and babies share another section. Houses made of mud with thatched roofs surround a central courtyard. It is a sleepover every night for Ghanaian teenagers living in compounds. Adults may have a separate room. In other cases, family members may occupy neighboring houses, which may be in the same compound.

In the past, the clan system encouraged large families for protection. Today tribal wars have ended, reducing the need for large numbers of fighters. The infant-death rate has declined. Although family-planning services have been available since 1966, many Ghanaians still prefer large families as a form of social and economic security.

Hanging out with Friends

In the past, because of close-knit families, parents exerted great influence on their teenagers' choices of friends. Like many aspects of family life, that is now changing. Today, teens in Ghana make friends for much the same reasons that teens worldwide do— because they like the same things and have fun together. Friends are made at school and in community settings. Parties, sports events, festivals, and even the marketplaces offer opportunities for making new friends. Teens are usually free to date whomever they choose. Most couples prefer group dates, rather than pairing off.

In traditional extended families, Ghanaian teenagers still have some social choices. However, parental influences and constraints limit their options. Busy school schedules, tutoring, working at part-time jobs, and family responsibilities dictate the amount of time teenagers spend with friends.

Some view the work of children as a source of additional family income. However, government leaders want to limit rapid population growth, which can use up resources. The government sponsors massive publicity and educational campaigns on family planning.

Older family members receive high respect from their kin. They are honored for their wisdom and life experiences. At social gatherings, the elderly are the first to be greeted, seated, and served. The elderly pass on traditional stories and teach traditional crafts to the young. They serve as advisers to teenagers, teaching them about morals and manners.

Minding Your Manners

In Ghana, the left hand is considered unclean. It is an insult to dip one's left hand into food. Gifts must never be accepted or given with the left hand. When shaking hands with Ghanaians, begin with the person on the right. Starting from the left is rude.

The Role of Women

Civil rights for women developed slowly in Ghana. In the 1980s, Ghana's high fertility rate of 6.9 showed that women's primary role was childbearing. Since then, the fertility rate has declined. The 2007 fertility rate for Ghana was estimated at 3.89 children. The rate is still above the world average of 2.59, but it is lower than in most other west African countries, including Nigeria (5.45), Liberia (5.94), and Sierra Leone (6.01).

Even so, the high risk of dying from pregnancy has not changed. There are 540 deaths for every 100,000 pregnancies. When compared with the rates of more developed countries, the ratio is incredibly high. In an effort to lower the ratio, the government provides free care for pregnant women.

The women of Ghana face other challenges as well. The 1992 constitution guarantees the basic rights of all Ghanaian citizens, but these rights are not always enforced. Few people are fully aware of women's rights under the law. Women suffer unfair treatment in employment, marriage, and divorce in particular. Polygamy (having multiple wives) is lawful under customary law. However, the practice places women in inferior positions. After their first marriage, men usually choose teens for second or third wives. Supporters of the practice believe that teens adapt to first wives more easily than older women do.

Ghana's Famous Son

Kofi Annan, the former secretary-general of the United Nations, is Ghana's most famous son. He was born in Kumasi in 1938. The name Kofi means "born on a Friday." His father was half Asante and half Fante; his mother belonged to the Fante tribe. Both of Annan's grandfathers and an uncle were tribal chiefs. Soft-spoken Annan learned about politics early from his family.

Annan studied in Kumasi, Minnesota, Massachusetts, and Switzerland before joining the United Nations in 1962. He worked as an administrative and budget officer with the World Health Organization. He became secretary-general of the United Nations in 1997, when the international organization was almost out of money. He is credited with renewing the organization. Annan is widely admired for his efforts on behalf of Africa, where the problems of war, famine, disease, and displaced people continue.

Kofi Annan returned home to Ghana in January 2007, after serving for 10 years as secretary-general. In June 2007, he became chairman of the Alliance for a Green Revolution in Africa, financed by the Bill and Melinda Gates Foundation and the Rockefeller Foundation. The aim of the alliance is to help small-scale farmers in Africa grow more crops.

Kofi Annan won the Nobel Peace Prize in 2001 for his work with the United Nations.

There have been successes for women. In 1985, for example, the government passed a law that protects women whose husbands die without a will. Traditionally the wife would lose the family property. The law keeps the land in the wife's hands.

More recently, the Ministry of Women and Children's Affairs was established in 2001. The ministry promotes the welfare of women and children in Ghana and tries to ensure equal status for women. In February 2007, Parliament passed the hotly debated Domestic Violence Bill. This law defines what abuse is, including threats and physical assault. Before the law, husbands who beat their wives could not be punished by law. When the bill was passed, female Parliament members

Champion for Human Rights

Lawyer Angela Dwamena-Aboagye, a 41-year-old married African woman with four children, works to support various causes affecting human rights in Ghana. She tries to free women and children from laws and practices that violate their rights. She established the first shelter for abused women and children in Ghana. She started an institute to provide learning opportunities for young female leaders. She also led the way in the creation of a legal and counseling crisis center for victims of human-rights abuse.

In 2005, Aboagye was one of 13 women from the continent to win the African Women of Substance Award. This award honors women who are working to make a difference in the lives of the vulnerable and the powerless. Also, she was one of 50 Ghanaian women featured in a 2006 photography exhibition, "Women Empowering Women." These women were honored for their efforts to strengthen the rights of children and women.

waved their handkerchiefs and embraced each other. Efforts are under way to explain and enforce these laws.

The idea of child rights is slowly gaining ground in Ghana. In 1998, the Children's Act was passed. This law puts forth the rights of the child and makes parental duties clear. The law provides for the care and protection of children. Abuse and exploitation (unfair treatment) of children still occur in Ghana. However, some progress has been made in various areas of child protection.

In January 2006, the United Nations released a report from the Committee on the Rights of the Child. The report noted that 39 percent of children in Ghana between the ages of 5 and 17 worked in mining, quarrying, fishing, or agriculture. Alima Mahama is the minister for women and children's affairs of Ghana. She said the government was "determined to do everything possible to improve the well-being and development of Ghanaian children." She cited areas still requiring attention, including poverty reduction, improved education for girls, and better health care. In addition, physical violence and neglect are major concerns. As the ministry gains funding, more programs will be added to work on children's problems.

Family Life in the Future

In recent years, changes in society have affected family life. The extended family remains a powerful influence. At the same time, the nuclear family is stronger than ever before. In cities and towns, strict parental control has eased. Modernization offers opportunities for teens to develop independence. In urban areas, the typical large family size has been reduced. Many parents now want both their sons and daughters to receive an education. These changes reflect the widening influence of global ideas. Ghanaians young and old strive to adapt to a modern way of life.

A young boy weaves mats that his mother will sell at a market. Though some work poses no physical danger to children, they still suffer from a lack of education.

A Man with a Mission

In Ghana, 10 percent of the population is disabled by deformities at birth or by disease. This portion of the population is considered cursed. At one time, many disabled children were left to die in the wilderness, abandoned by their parents. Today, the disabled are often concealed from the public eye by ashamed family members. Or they are thrown into the public eye to spend a lifetime begging on the streets.

In 1977, Emmanuel Ofosu Yeboah was born in Koforidua with a severely deformed right leg. His parents lived in a farming village, in a primitive compound that had no electricity or running water. His father, ashamed of his son's deformity, abandoned the family. Instead of concealing Yeboah at home or sending him to the streets to beg, his mother raised him alone—and even sent him to school.

Though he faced ridicule in school, he managed to become an athlete. His mother taught him to believe that he deserved the same privileges as able-bodied Ghanaians. In his early teens, he left school when his mother became too ill to support the family. Too proud to beg, Yeboah learned to shine shoes. With his crutches, a box to sit on, and tools to shine shoes, he left home to work on the streets of Accra. After a couple of months, he returned home with money to support his mother.

After his mother's death, Yeboah felt compelled to share with the nation the message he had learned from his mother—that disability does not mean inability. In an effort to reach the more than 2 million citizens with disabilities, he decided to ride a bicycle across Ghana. Yeboah had mastered pedaling with only one leg, but there was another obstacle. He didn't own a bike.

A missionary in Accra put Yeboah in touch with the California-based Challenged Athletes Foundation. The foundation donated a mountain bike and other equipment for his journey. In July 2002, he set out on a bike trip across his country. Stories about his journey appeared in newspapers and aired on the radio. By the end of the trip, he had become a national hero.

Yeboah has turned his disability into a tool to help others. Since the cross-country bike ride, he has been fitted with a prosthetic leg that allows him to stand on both feet. Also, he has helped to provide free wheelchairs to benefit Ghana's disabled, and he worked for the passage of a disabilities law. In 2005, he was the subject of a movie. *Emmanuel's Gift,* an award-winning documentary, showcased Yeboah's passion and vision. Almost one year later, the Parliament of Ghana passed the Persons with Disability bill. The law gives the disabled the same rights, such as equal employment opportunities, given to able-bodied citizens by Ghana's constitution.

In 2005, Yeboah was honored with two awards: the ESPY Arthur Ashe Courage award and the Nike Casey Martin award.

Teens enjoy festivals and celebrations as both performers and observers.

4

Land of Festivals

GHANAIANS LOVE HAVING FUN AND CELEBRATING THEIR CULTURE. More than 100 festivals take place in Ghana throughout the year. Though diverse in nature, the festivals have a common purpose. They are held to remember past leaders and to gain a sense of renewal. All festivals involve colorful displays, music and dance, and great feasting. The festivals are closely tied to the traditional religions that existed in Ghana—and still do, to a certain extent—before the emergence of Christianity and Islam.

Traditional religions include belief in a supreme being or god who created the world. Followers also believe that the things around them, such as trees and mountains, have spirits. The spirits of ancestors are also believed to surround the living. Modern festivals acknowledge the tribe's belief in the spirit world. They serve as a symbolic link between the living and the dead. Through festivals, Ghanaians pass cultural traditions from one generation to another.

Thousands of people from all walks of life, including

foreigners, come to Ghana to see tribal festivals. Once there, they are greeted by the famous hospitality and friendliness of Ghanaians. A large number of festival goers are teenagers. City teenagers often travel long distances to their home villages to attend the festivals and connect with their kin. Festivals also provide opportunities for making new friends. Typical festival activities appeal to teens, and the young people are often invited to participate. They take part in physical exercises and re-enactments of historical events, for example. But for most teens, the best part of a festival is the music and dancing, both traditional and modern.

Tribal Chiefs

The tribal system of government in Ghana has outlasted military governments, civilian governments, and British rule. In ancient times, each tribe had its own chief, who ruled in his area with the help of a council of elders. During British colonial rule, the chief's position tended to follow the central government's position. Since independence in 1957, the various Ghanaian governments have kept the tribal system but gradually reduced its ruling powers.

Tribal chiefs still play a major role in the lives of Ghanaians, particularly those living in rural areas. The 1992 constitution protects the institution of chieftaincy and allows for customary and traditional councils. Tribal chiefs govern over customs and tribal matters, such as interpreting traditional law and settling local disputes. Even so, the role of the tribal chiefs today is largely ceremonial.

Major Festivals

Each ethnic group has its own distinctive festivals. Many festivals follow the cycle of the seasons. Some festivals mark the start of a new year. These involve cleaning out the house and clearing the land for the planting of crops. Others pay honor to ancestors. Some festivals celebrate the arrival of the tribe in Ghana. No matter what the focus, every festival is celebrated with traditional music, dance, art, feasts, and tributes to ancestors.

The Akans celebrate the Odwira harvest festival to give thanks for the new crop of yams. This weeklong festival is also a time of mourning for members who died during the past year. Akans also use this time to pay tribute to ancestors for their guidance. It is held in September or October, depending on the harvest.

Special celebrations and rituals occur each day of Odwira. On

Monday, the path to the royal mausoleum (a stately tomb) is swept. Tuesday is the day for eating new yams. On Wednesday, the Akans fast and mourn the dead. In contrast, Thursday is the day of feasting. People are free to visit any home, including the chief's palace, to eat. That night people stay inside their houses because they believe their ancestors are walking the streets. The next day is a day of celebration.

On Saturday comes the durbar. This colorful procession of tribal chiefs is the highlight of all Ghanaian festivals. For this occasion, the chiefs dress in their finest ceremonial robes, accentuated in glittering gold. They sit in big wooden seats, called palanquins. Here they are shaded from the sun by huge velvet-fringed umbrellas of brilliant colors. Four to six men carry the heavy, decorated palanquins on their shoulders through streets lined with people. The parade is a noisy, colorful event.

Traditional durbars last a whole day, ending with a procession from the public grounds to the high chief's palace. At the end, the high chief receives honors as he sits surrounded by lesser chiefs and elders. Special guests extend

The procession of the durbar is often accompanied by drumming, singing, and dancing.

greetings to the chiefs, and gifts are presented. Special drinks are shared to honor ancestors and give thanks to the supreme creator.

The Odwira festival concludes on Sunday with a day of worship and giving thanks to the gods.

The Ga people celebrate their own harvest festival, called Homowo, which translates to "hooting or mocking hunger." Each year the Ga gather, from far and near, in their homeland near the Greater Accra region to observe this ritual. The festival is related to the traditional occupations of Ga society—farming and fishing.

According to oral history, there was a time hundreds of years ago when the rains stopped. Lack of rain resulted in a famine that spread throughout the southern Accra Plains, causing many deaths. After a long time, the rains returned, crops were planted, and food became plentiful again. Overjoyed, the Ga people celebrated with a festival that made fun of hunger.

Homowo dances follow the ritual feast. The dances begin with the chiefs hooting at hunger by drumming on their knees with their hands. Then everyone joins in the joyful, jostling dances. Teens are in the forefront of the merrymaking. The Day of Remembrance follows the feasting and dancing. It serves as a time to remember the ties between the dead and living. It is also a time to wish family and friends well during the coming year.

Another popular tribal festival is the Fante festival of Aboakyer. Falling in May, this festival is believed to be more than 300 years old. The celebration attracts people from around the globe to the coastal city of Winneba. Various sports activities take place, including a regatta (boat race), a cross country race, football (soccer) games, and beach volleyball. Teens love the sports events.

This festival is also known as the "deer catching" festival. Two groups compete to be the first to find and catch a deer in the forests around Winneba. Only sticks and short clubs can be used in catching the deer.

A priestess makes an offering to the dead. Various customary rituals are performed as part of Homowo.

Religion in Ghana

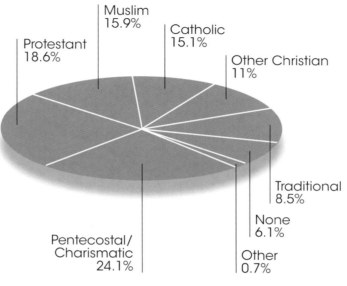

Protestant
18.6%

Muslim
15.9%

Catholic
15.1%

Other Christian
11%

Traditional
8.5%

None
6.1%

Other
0.7%

Pentecostal/
Charismatic
24.1%

Source: United States Central Intelligence Agency.
The World Factbook—Ghana.

Each side has its own unique colors and flags. The chief performs a purification ceremony at the beach before the groups set out to catch the deer. Once the deer is caught, it is sacrificed to the gods. Afterward, the head priest tells the community of the gods' predictions for the coming year.

Some festivals combine traditional beliefs with other religions, such as Islam. Most people in the northern regions of Ghana celebrate the annual Damba festival. Originally an Islamic festival, it is now celebrated by Muslims and non-Muslims alike. Held in August,

it is actually two festivals. First, Somba Damba marks the birth of the Prophet Muhammad. The second festival is called Naa Damba and celebrates the naming of Muhammad. Both festivals combine traditional rituals, such as paying tribute to ancestors, with Islamic prayers and the reading of the Qur'an. The long celebration, with its drum-playing, dancing, and feasting, is an enjoyable time for the people living in the northern regions.

Traditional Rituals
In addition to festivals, Ghanaians perform rituals throughout the year.

Afehyia Pa!

Ghana is a predominantly Christian country. So Christmas is one of the most important and joyous religious festivals. It lasts for many days. Throughout the celebration, people cry out *"Afehyia Pa"*—"Merry Christmas and a Happy New Year." All Ghanaians, no matter their tribal affiliation, use this cheery Akan greeting. Radio and television stations play Christmas music. Holiday shoppers jam decorated city streets.

Afehyia Pa
ah-FEH-hyah pah

Christmas in Ghana is a time when relatives and friends visit each other. They travel from town to town and village to village in cars, buses, and trucks displaying Christmas decorations. Many rush back to their hometowns or villages by Christmas Eve. After the traditional Christmas Eve church worship service, there is usually a procession through the streets led by local bands. Dancing in the streets continues until the wee hours of the morning.

On Christmas Day, people return to church wearing their finest clothes. The Christmas story is retold in ethnic languages, and carols are sung. After the service, people usually gather in homes for a special Christmas Day feast. Colorful crepe paper gives a festive look to the houses. Christmas ornaments, usually made of paper, decorate a mango or palm tree. Christmas Day dinners may include rice, chicken, goat, lamb, vegetables, and fruits of all kinds, such as mangoes, oranges, or bananas. Families exchange gifts, and children also receive gifts brought by Father Christmas, or Santa Claus. Children in rural areas receive practical gifts, such as new clothes, soap, or a book. In contrast, children in urban areas receive expensive toys and electronic gadgets.

In some areas of Ghana, celebrants dress in costumes and masks and visit others on Christmas.

52

A ritual ceremony marks the taking on of a new role in a society. From birth to death, each person goes through certain rites of passage. Naming a child, entering puberty, and getting married are all marked with rites.

When a baby is born, the child and mother stay inside for seven days after the birth. On the eighth day, the naming ceremony, also called "outdooring," begins with placing the baby on the ground. The crowd gathers around for the ceremony. The baby is usually given an ancestor's name and a name that coordinates with the day of the week on which the baby was born. The priest or family elder prays. He asks blessings for all who are gathered. Special prayers are said for the baby. A grand feast with singing and dancing follows the ceremony.

The next major stage in a person's life is the transition to adulthood. For girls, this is the time they are taught the skills needed for adult life.

Traditional Ghanaian Names

A person's name is believed to influence his or her character. Naming children takes special care. Akans name their children according to which day of the week they were born. Every Ghanaian's name has at least two parts. The first part comes from the day of birth and the baby's gender. Thus, a baby born on Friday is called Kofi (male) or Afua (female). The second part of the name is the father's name. A family name is another option for the second name. The father chooses a name from an ancestral list of names.

	Boy	Girl
Monday	Kojo	Adwoa
Tuesday	Kobina	Abena
Wednesday	Kwaku	Akua
Thursday	Yaw	Aba /Yaa
Friday	Kofi	Afua
Saturday	Kwame	Ama
Sunday	Kwasi	Esi/Akosua

They also learn how to act morally, according to cultural expectations. Folklore, games, and practical experiences make the learning fun. Initiation rites emphasize domestic skills, such as cooking, cleaning, and caring for children. In the past, initiation rites were quite elaborate, but today they are simple. However, they still mark an important stage of a girl's life.

One traditional puberty rite, known as female genital mutilation (FMG), negatively affects women's health in Ghana. Part or all of the girl's clitoris is removed, often resulting in physical and emotional trauma. The procedures are often performed by village elders or traditional birth attendants.

FMG was made illegal in 1994. Those who perform the procedure can be sentenced to at least three years in prison. Nonetheless, the practice remains common among groups in the northern regions of the country and among groups of migrants from the north living in the Accra area. They claim that the practice is a requirement for marriage. But doctors say that females who have this type of surgery are likely to experience problems during childbirth. Governmental efforts to combat female genital mutilation continue.

Boys also undergo initiation rites intended to prepare them to become responsible adults. In the past, many of the boys received guns as a symbol of their readiness to hunt and join in the defense of their village. Today the focus

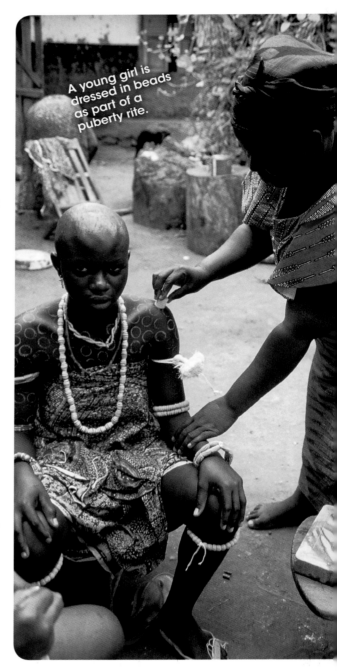

A young girl is dressed in beads as part of a puberty rite.

LAND OF FESTIVALS

is learning how to fulfill their duties to society. Often boys are taken outside of town. There they undergo physical-endurance tests and participate in competitive sports. The boys are also taught basic job skills as part of the rituals. These skills are designed to enable boys to support themselves and their families during adulthood.

Love & Marriage

Marriage remains the most important social institution in Ghana. The significance of marrying and having children made arranged marriages common at one time. In these marriages the couple's parents chose suitable partners for their children. The marriages linked two families for political or economic reasons. Love was not a factor. Today men and women often choose their own partners. Even so, marriage continues to revolve around much more than the bride and groom. It is still mainly the union of two families.

The legal age for marriage in Ghana is 18 for females and 21 for males. There are three types of marriage—statutory, customary, and religious. A statutory ceremony is performed by a government official. It is a somewhat new trend, chosen mostly by educated people in towns and cities who prefer a civil marriage.

By far more common are customary marriages, also called traditional marriages. Even people who marry in a church often are married first in a

The groom's family gives the bride's family a gift of money as part of a customary ceremony.

customary ceremony. Family members play a major role in these ceremonies, and teens often serve as members of the wedding party. Customary weddings are normally held at the bride's family home. At the start of the ceremony, before the bride appears, the groom's family gives gifts, known as brideswealth, to the bride's family. Wedding guests enjoy watching, and the atmosphere is filled with fun. When the business is complete, the bride finally appears. The couple signs their marriage license, a minister blesses their union, and, with the ceremony complete, refreshments are served.

Christian weddings in Ghana feature elements of Western weddings. One visitor to Ghana attended such a wedding. She said:

The wedding I went to was supposed to start at noon but did not begin until two. Everyone, except me, was dressed in beautiful Ghanaian bright silk fabrics. The place was packed. There is no such thing as a small Ghanaian wedding. You do not have to be invited to attend. If you hear that a friend of yours is getting married, you should attend. The wedding itself was over three hours long. Then the reception was just an extension of the wedding with speeches and songs and lasted for at least another hour.

Final Goodbyes

Death is considered the final rite of passage. Ghanaians view death as a transition from the physical world to the spiritual world. Funeral ceremonies are a time for the people of a community to come together. Huge amounts of money are spent on funerals. Most believe that no expense should be spared.

Wedding Gifts

Brideswealth, the gifts given by the groom's family to the bride's family, represent each family's approval of the other. The acceptance of the gifts formalizes the marriage contract. Brideswealth is in no way payment for the sale of a female into marriage, and it is not compensation for labor lost. Brideswealth is a symbol of gratitude and appreciation to the family for allowing their daughter to marry. It creates a physical bond between the two families, as well as a symbolic bond.

Brideswealth may include bottles of liquor, pots of palm wine, kola nuts, and money. In some cases, the groom's family presents the traditional gifts of cattle, goats, and chickens. Often the amount of the brideswealth is substantial and serves to enhance the commitment of both families.

Elaborate coffins can cost from 2.3 million to 14 million Ghanaian cedis (U.S.$250 to $1,500).

In Ghana, coffin-making is considered an art form. It is common to make a coffin depicting the life of the deceased. A fisherman's coffin may be a huge tuna carved out of wood and painted. A tribal chief may be buried in an eagle-shaped coffin. A rich man may order a coffin in the shape of a Mercedes-Benz. In addition to the coffin, the costs of special clothing, food, drinks, and music often place families in financial trouble.

Funerals are held on weekends. The wake begins on Friday and usually lasts all night. During this time, mourners keep watch over the body, and eat and drink together. The burial and funeral rites take place on Saturday. Often the service continues through Sunday. No matter the circumstances, funerals are a solemn event. The service is accompanied by funeral songs. While there is much wailing by females, men do not show their emotions in public. It is not proper. Additional rituals are designed to complete the journey of the deceased. These take place after the funeral rites.

National Holidays

National holidays are joyous times for the people of Ghana. They feature cultural activities and entertainment that appeal to teenagers. Holidays include traditional and modern styles of music and dance. In coastal areas, people flock to the beaches on holidays.

One of the most important holidays is Independence Day, held on March 6. This is the anniversary of the day Ghanaians gained their freedom from Great Britain in 1957. The year 2007 marked Ghana's 50th anniversary as a country. Many celebrations were held to mark the occasion, with three goals in mind. First, organizers wanted to celebrate and commemorate Ghana's being the first black country in Africa to attain independence from colonial rule. They also saw the anniversary as an opportunity to reflect on the country's achievements and challenges over the past 50 years. Finally they wanted Ghanaians to look forward to the future.

Weeks before the big day arrived, authorities in Accra began clearing the city's business district of unauthorized buildings and street vendors as part of a massive cleanup. Policemen on horses guarded the market streets, and hawkers were kept away until the festivities were over. A new market awaited visitors. Throughout the country, celebrations showed a beautiful Ghana to guests, including leaders from around the world.

Public Holidays

There are 12 public holidays in Ghana. The dates of holidays that are religious in origin are set according to their respective lunar calendars (calendars based on the moon's motion). As a result, the dates vary from year to year.

New Year's Day—January 1
Eid-al-Adha—Islamic holiday
Independence Day—March 6
Good Friday—Christian holiday
Easter Monday—Christian holiday
May Day (Worker's Day)—May 1
African Union Day—May 25
Republic Day—July 1
Eid-al-Fitr—Islamic holiday
Farmer's Day—First Friday in December
Christmas Day—December 25
Boxing Day—December 26

Independence & Beyond

Ghanaians take special pride in celebrating their Independence Day. Perhaps this is because they have faced many struggles in their first 50 years of freedom.

On March 6, 1957, Ghana became the first sub-Saharan country to end colonial rule. On this date, Britain transferred power to independence leader Kwame Nkrumah as prime minister. In 1960, a new constitution created the Republic of Ghana and gave people the right to elect representatives to exercise power for them. That same year, Ghanaians elected Nkrumah president of Ghana.

Opposition to Nkrumah grew in the early 1960s. Many Ghanaians blamed his ambitious programs for their economic hardships. He tried to do too much too fast. Without enough money to fund the projects, the government resorted to taking out loans and borrowing money from other countries. The new nation was drowning in debt. In 1966, Nkrumah was overthrown by a military coup. A series of unstable governments—civilian and military—ran Ghana after that, with one coup after another.

In 1992, a new constitution called for an elected parliament as well as a chief executive officer. It also allowed for a multiparty political system. In 1992, Ghanaians elected Flight Lieutenant Jerry Rawlings president. At the same time, elections for the 200-member national Parliament were held. Rawlings retired in 2000 after stabilizing a turbulent political scene and leading the country on a path toward economic recovery.

The swearing in of John Kufuor as president in January 2001 marked the first time since Ghana's independence that power had changed hands peacefully and democratically.

Thousands of teen girls work as porters, carrying goods on their heads. The work is difficult and can cause pain.

5

The Challenge of Child Labor

A TEENAGER SHINES SHOES IN ACCRA. HIS MEAGER EARNINGS—LESS THAN 2 CEDIS (U.S.$2.13) A DAY—provide for no more than a mere existence on the streets. Two years ago, he dropped out of school and left his Ashanti village. Telling no one, he just walked away. There would be one less mouth to feed in his family. He walked for days. Finally, he caught a crowded truck to Accra. Hungry and bewildered, the young boy reached the big city. He soon realized the misery of life on the streets. During the first week, he suffered beatings by other street boys and even the police. His first job was in a street market, hauling away garbage. After two months, he landed a job shining shoes. Now 14 years of age, the boy thinks of becoming an apprentice in metalworking. In the meantime, he continues to shine shoes.

Throughout Ghana, teens work to contribute to the family income or to support themselves. In some cases, teens assist in family businesses, working as clerks or salespeople. Some assist with farm labor. Other teens help their families by selling produce in markets.

Some teens go into traditional occupations. They spend long hours learning craft skills, such as weaving and jewelry-making. It takes dedication to become a carpenter, mason, blacksmith, or woodcarver. Some modern occupations, such as bicycle repair,

The traditional stool is among the most recognizable and popular products of Ghanaian woodcarvers.

require apprenticeships. As a result of vocational training, many teens find jobs in manufacturing.

However, there is a dark side to the picture. Not all teens are fortunate enough to obtain the training that is required for these kinds of jobs. Efforts to combat rising levels of poverty have met with little success. More than 30 percent of Ghana's population falls below the poverty line. In some areas, the poverty rates range as high as 80 percent. Most poor people live in rural areas.

Child labor is a serious problem in Ghana. A recent government study revealed there are 1.5 million Ghanaian children under the age of 15 who have dropped out of school to work. It is illegal for children under 15 to be employed. Yet child labor is widespread. Most of these workers are in their early to mid teens and come from poverty-stricken rural areas.

The survey also showed that children and teenagers are often required to work in harmful conditions. Ghana Police Superintendent Elizabeth Dassah noted that the most alarming finding of the survey was "the fact that even though the minimum age of employment in hazardous labor was 18 years, children as young as 5 to 17 years were engaged in this nature of work."

Street Children

Each day, the number of teenagers moving from a rural area to a major city rises. Most end up in Kumasi or Accra. There are many reasons for leaving home, including poverty, abuse, family breakup, and parental death. The lure of the cities is the possibility of a job and a chance for adventure. Once they arrive, their dreams end abruptly. Jobs are hard to find.

An estimated 20,000 street children end up in Accra. Many work in dangerous situations. The hours are long, and the pay is low. At night, they sleep in

Who Are They?

The United Nations defines street children as boys and girls who call the street home or earn their living on the street without responsible adult protection or supervision. This broad definition includes homeless children who live on the street. Young people who work on the street and earn just enough money for food are also considered street children. This definition does not include children who live on the street with their families.

63

doorways or alleys. They lack a proper diet. Their hygiene is poor. They have no access to health care. And they do not attend school. On the street, teenagers risk abuse and arrest. Girls face the danger of rape and other sexual abuse.

Porters of Ghana

In Accra and Kumasi, many of the children on the street are teenage girls. Most are from the northern areas of Ghana. They leave home because their families don't have the money to provide for them. On the street, they are known as *kayayei* girls. This is a local term for female porters. They band together and form their own miniature communities.

As porters, these girls cling to their oversized tin bowls, their most prized possession. They use the tin bowls to carry loads of goods, balanced on their

kayayei
kay-a-YOO

Benches in the Tamale Market make beds for street children.

heads. During the day, these girls roam the streets dressed in flowing gauze skirts and flip-flops. Customers tip the porters for transporting loads, but the girls earn barely enough for food. They sleep huddled in their tin bowls along the storefronts at night.

Rescuing Street Children

The Kumasi Street Children Project, a nongovernmental organization (NGO), addresses the living conditions of street life. Volunteers run the project, which now sponsors more than 140 children rescued from the street. These children have been sent to school. Some are receiving vocational training. Funding comes from grants and contributions from private donors.

Youth Alive serves the northern regions of Ghana. This NGO works to help teenagers stay with their families. Funding is limited, but the volunteers hope to reverse a cycle of street life that involves generation after generation.

Fifteen-year-old Issah is a boy porter. He came from Bolgatanga in the Upper East Region of Ghana and has been working on the streets for the past year. He said:

I dropped out of Primary 3 because my father said I had to take the cows out to graze. I couldn't combine school with looking after cattle. One day … I took my father's bicycle. … One of my little brothers came with me. When I got there [to the bus station], I bought a bus ticket and told my brother to take the bicycle back home. … I arrived in Kumasi around 6 A.M. I didn't know anyone here.

Though he struggled at first, Issah now has regular customers. He is one of the lucky ones. He is able to save some of his money. Also, he does not sleep on the streets. He cleans the bus station in exchange for a place to sleep inside. He dreams of setting up a television and video shop in Kumasi.

Harmful Work

Ghana places high value on teens who work at home or on the family farm. There is a strong belief that working is good for the child. It helps develop skills and a sense of responsibility. Though it helps meet a family's financial needs, child labor can rob a teenager of an education and the opportunities that education brings. Lack of education is not only harmful to the individual but also to society itself.

Nearly one in three Ghanaian

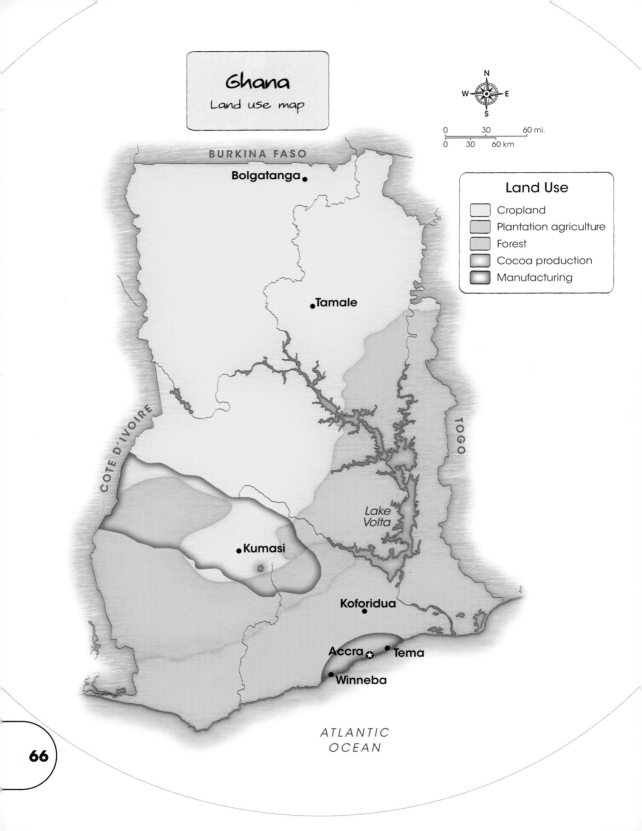

Ghana
Land use map

N
W E
S

0   30   60 mi.
0   30   60 km

BURKINA FASO

Bolgatanga

Land Use
Cropland
Plantation agriculture
Forest
Cocoa production
Manufacturing

Tamale

CÔTE D'IVOIRE

TOGO

Lake
Volta

Kumasi

Koforidua

Accra Tema
Winneba

ATLANTIC
OCEAN

children under 15 work in agriculture. Some of the work, such as cocoa farming, is dangerous. Research shows that 64 percent of children who work on cocoa farms are under 14. A majority of the children use large, heavy knives called machetes to clear fields. Children can suffer accidents as a result of using the machetes. Others apply chemicals known as pesticides without using protective gear. Many children pick cocoa pods. To remove the cocoa beans, they use sharp knives to open the pods.

In May 2000, the Ghana National Commission expressed concern about the dangers of child labor in inland fishing. This practice was found in 156 fishing villages around Lake Volta and the River Volta. Young children dive down to the riverbeds to free tangled nets. The threat of children's falling out of boats is constant, and reports of their drowning

Manufacturing & Industry

Although Ghana's economy is based mainly on agriculture, the industrial sector plays an important role by producing goods from local products. Ghana's food-processing industries include sugar refineries, flour mills, and a few cocoa-processing factories that make Ghanaian chocolate. Also, there are beef-processing plants, milk-processing factories, and pineapple factories. Vegetable-oil mills produce coconut and palm oil. Ghanaian-grown cotton is processed into cloth and then into clothes in factories.

The forests of Ghana contribute to another vital industry—timber. About 70,000 people work in that industry. About 250,000 more work in related fields, such as milling and manufacturing.

The industrial city of Tema is home to an aluminum processing plant, an iron and steel plant, and a petroleum refinery. Chemical plants make paint, pesticides, and medicines. Although there is a small gold-processing plant in Ghana, most of the raw material is exported.

67

The Cocoa Cash Crop

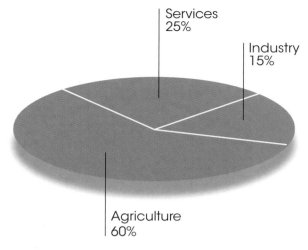

Services 25%

Industry 15%

Agriculture 60%

Source: United States Central Intelligence Agency. *The World Factbook—Ghana.*

In 1878, a Ghanaian brought cocoa beans from South America into the country, introducing what is now Ghana's top cash crop. Cocoa grows in the forest regions of central Ghana. The tropical conditions—high heat, abundant rainfall, elevated humidity, well-drained soil, and shade from the high forest trees—make for an ideal growing environment. It takes five years for cocoa trees to become productive.

Harvesting can take four or five months, beginning in September. Collecting the large, ripe pods and scooping out the beans require many workers because the labor is done by hand. In the next stage, the beans ferment for several days. Then the beans are sun-dried for about two weeks before being packed into bags for shipment.

In June 2007, agriculture giant Archer Daniels Midland Co. announced the building of a cocoa processing facility with the latest technology in Kumasi. The company decided to locate in Kumasi to be closer to the cocoa farmers and provide jobs to the community.

are numerous. News reports have pointed out the increasing number of young boys in the fishing business. They work in exchange for a small yearly payment to their parents. This practice provides fishermen with cheap labor.

What Does the Future Hold?

The Children's Act of 1998 set the minimum age of employment in Ghana at 15. This act also banned abusive child labor. However, the law has been ineffective because of the lack of money to enforce it. Another problem has been lack of awareness on the part of parents. They do not realize their children face dangerous conditions. Cocoa farmers who

Critics of child labor in Ghana's fishing industry consider the forced labor a modern form of slavery.

hire teenagers run the risk of criminal charges. But charging them with a crime is difficult because so many teenagers do not have a birth certificate to prove their age. Efforts to register all children without birth certificates are continuing.

In 2006, a video showed rescues of child laborers in the fishing villages of Ghana. Children in the video ranged in age from 5 to 16. They were recovering in a government shelter. There they received food, health care, and counseling. Programs are under way to help parents raise their income and send their children to school. The hope is for a safer future for the children.

Ghana was the first country to approve the United Nations Convention on the Rights of the Child in 1990. By doing so, Ghana recognized that children are exposed to danger. The government also recognized that children require special protection. In a speech on children's rights, President John Kufuor said, "What many of you do not know is that violence and the abuse of children result in serious socio-economic health, as well as psychological, consequences" that hurt the development of children.

One popular pastime in Ghana is practicing styles—a combination of break dancing, gymnastics, and acrobatics.

CHAPTER SIX

The Sights & Sounds of Ghana

IT'S A FRIDAY AFTERNOON IN ACCRA. THE SKIES ARE A STUNNING BLUE. At the West Africa Secondary School, teenagers stream out the doorways. The weekend has arrived! A keen listener catches words and phrases above the noise. Talk of football games, boxing matches, discos, cyber cafes, video theaters, music, and text messages fills the air. Everyone has plans for the weekend. There is much to see and do in this coastal country, with its astonishing array of attractions.

Lying just north of the equator, Ghana is a tropical country. The year-round average temperature is about 79 degrees Fahrenheit (26 degrees Celsius), and Ghana experiences dry and wet seasons. The rainy seasons fall from March to July and from September to November. In between, Ghanaians enjoy hours and hours of sunshine. Teenagers make good use of the warm climate. Outdoor activities go on throughout the year. Ghana provides a wide variety of leisure activities for teens.

In general, teens value leisure and entertainment time. Urban and rural teenagers enjoy spending time with others. They cherish the time spent sharing stories and playing games. They are open to new experiences.

Sports & Games

Whether playing or watching, teenagers love sports. As in many other African countries, football is Ghana's national sport. It commands a huge following and is a topic of lively conversations. Everyone is an expert on the subject!

Boys play football with any round object available. They set up football fields in open spaces. A short version of football is played on city streets. It is called "gutter to gutter" ball. Every young boy dreams of playing for the Black Stars, Ghana's national team.

For many years, Ghanaian girls

Go, Team, Go!

Ghanaians proudly cheer for the Black Stars, the senior national football team of Ghana. Stephen Appiah, an attacking midfielder, is a star of the team. The 26-year-old is no stranger to international competition. He appeared in three world championships at the junior level during his teens. The Black Stars qualified for the World Cup finals for the first time in January 2006. Appiah made the African Nations Cup All-Star team in February 2006. In June 2006, he received the Man of the Match award after Ghana's World Cup match victory against the United States.

Stephen Appiah (in red) is known as the "Black Tornado."

did not play football. It was taboo. But today women have their own national football team, the Black Queens, which has played in the African Women's championship.

Boxing is another popular sport. Missionaries introduced it during the colonial period. They thought boxing would be a good physical activity that would keep teenage males off the streets. One of Ghana's greatest boxers was Azumah Nelson. The three-time world champion retired in 1998 after a boxing career that spanned 19 years.

Ghanaian teenagers take part in track and field events. They compete at regional and national levels. Almost every school holds competitions in these events. Sprinters have won international competitions. They have also fared well at the Olympics.

Urban teens find many other ways to relax and stay fit. Tennis, jogging, and working out in fitness clubs are all popular. Polo clubs are popular with the horse-racing crowd in Accra. Hiking clubs are for the hardy.

With miles of sandy ocean beaches, one might expect to see people enjoying the surf. This is not the case. Strong currents and tides make swimming dangerous. But swimming pools can be found in resorts just yards away from the ocean. Teens love to visit water parks on weekends and holidays. Waterskiing on Lake Volta attracts many teens as well. Lake Volta is one of the world's largest man-made lakes. The area of the lake measures 3,275 square miles (8,515 sq km). In addition to providing a place for recreation, Lake Volta generates electricity and allows transportation.

Ghanaians of all ages in rural

A favorite activity among Ashanti boys is racing while pushing wheels on long poles.

oware
oh-WAHR-ay

and urban areas play board games. They derive hours of pleasure from a board game called *oware*. Though exact rules for the game vary from region to region, it is played with 48 small objects (marbles or stones) on a board. The board has two rows of six holes (cups) on each side. In some rural areas, six holes dug in the sand serve as a board.

The goal is to move the game pieces around the board. The winner captures the opponent's game pieces. Experienced players move the game pieces faster than the eye can follow. Africans of all ages and skill levels have played this game, under many names, for thousands of years. Ancient Egyptians called it mancala, a name that is known to many of today's game players worldwide.

Leisure Pursuits

Teens in rural communities do not have the same recreational facilities as those in urban areas. Lack of electricity and money limits the types of activities available. But rural teens excel at improvising fun activities. For example, they do not have access to dance clubs. But the courtyards in the compounds are fine for dancing and games. In addition, boys hunt and fish as recreation.

In contrast, urban areas offer a wide variety of teen activities. These include video bars, cyber cafes, movies, parks, and discos. Economic differences dictate the types of activities in which teens participate.

Many teens spend time in city libraries. They provide a place to gather

Games such as oware are played as part of festivals.

Frequent Internet cafe users do everything from conducting business to online dating.

on weekends and holidays. Teens go to do research and homework, but libraries are also places to meet friends. For teens who are banned from dating, it is a good place to "date" without breaking the rules.

Teens can keep up with local and global news in libraries. They read newspapers such as *The Daily Graphic* and *The Ghanaian Chronicle*. Ghana enjoys a high degree of media freedom, with few restrictions on private publishers and broadcasters.

Libraries also stock books by local writers. Many of them write about their personal experiences. Ama Ata Aidoo is a poet, playwright, and novelist who writes about the struggles of Ghanaian women. She has also written about the corruption of government in the early years of independence. Her works include *Our Sister Killjoy* and *No Sweetness Here*. Kofi Awoonor also writes about life in Ghana. His book *Comes the Voyager at Last* is a moving tale of slavery. Anthony Kwamiah Johnson writes children's books, teenage novels, and adult fiction. His books include *Sunset at Noon* and *A Child of Nature*.

Award-winning Author

Meshack Asare is one of Ghana's favorite children's writers and illustrators. He has won many awards, including the Noma Award for Publishing in Africa (1982) for his *Kwajo and the Brassman's Secret*. He won the UNESCO First Prize for Children and Young People's Literature in the Service of Tolerance (1999) for *Sosu's Call*. This book, the story of a disabled boy who cannot walk, also placed in the top 12 of Africa's 100 Best Books of the 20th century.

Asare was born in Ghana near Cape Coast in 1945. As a child he listened to his grandparents and an uncle tell stories about his Ashanti heritage. He went on to study fine arts at the College of Art in Kumasi. He also taught school in Ghana for 12 years. It was during this period that he started to write and illustrate children's books. His other publications include *I Am Kofi, Tawia Goes to Sea, The Magic Goat, Nana's Son, Meliga's Day,* and *Noma's Sand*. His works have been translated and published in many foreign languages, including Japanese, Dutch, German, Russian, and Swedish.

Movies are a major form of entertainment for teenagers. They watch Chinese, Indian, Nigerian, European, and American films. Ghanaian-made films attract a wide audience, but the most popular films are American. No doubt, lifestyles and fashions in Hollywood films influence the pop culture of Ghana, from clothing to music choices.

In some areas, video theaters have replaced movie theaters because they are easier to get to and are cheaper. The requirements for video theaters are simple. All that's needed is a room (attached to a house or separate building), a television, and a VCR or DVD player. Video theaters seem to spring up on every corner. Teens flock to them with their friends to watch mainly Ghanaian and Western movies. The films explore themes such as class and gender issues, relationships, and economic problems. After the showing, people stick around to discuss the films.

For Ghanaian teenagers, watching television is a source of entertainment. They watch programming from local networks. And via satellite, they can see *The Oprah Winfrey Show* and American soap operas. CNN and other news channels provide information about what is going on in the world outside their own environment. Teens have a keen interest in global affairs.

Music & Dance
Music is an important part of every

Ghanaian's life. Important occasions are celebrated with music and dance. Listening to Ghanaian music is a popular recreational activity for teens as well. They enjoy a variety of music and dance.

There are three main types of music: ethnic (or traditional), highlife, and choral. Ethnic music is passed down through generations and is played during festivals and ceremonies. Highlife blends traditional and "imported" music for a more modern sound. Choral music, including hymns and gospel music, is performed in concert halls, churches, schools, and colleges.

Of the three, the most popular music in Ghana is highlife. The modern sounds appeal to young and old alike. Influenced by American swing and jazz, this vibrant music blends electric guitars and keyboards with African wooden drums. Sounds of traditional wind instruments, trumpets, and trombones add to highlife melodies. Most highlife songs are sung in the dialect of the Akan tribe. Some lyrics tell stories about daily life. Others are based on Ghanaian proverbs.

Highlife began in the coastal towns of Ghana in the 1920s. It had spread around the world by the 1950s. Accra-born musician King Bruce composed classic highlife songs and released many hits during the 1950s and 1990s. (The years in between, he worked in civil service and taught music.) Today the most popular highlife musician is Alex Konadu. He claims to have performed in every town and village in Ghana, and no one seems to doubt it. This dance music blends European ballroom with traditional Ghanaian dance. Teens love

Traditional music often features drums and vocals.

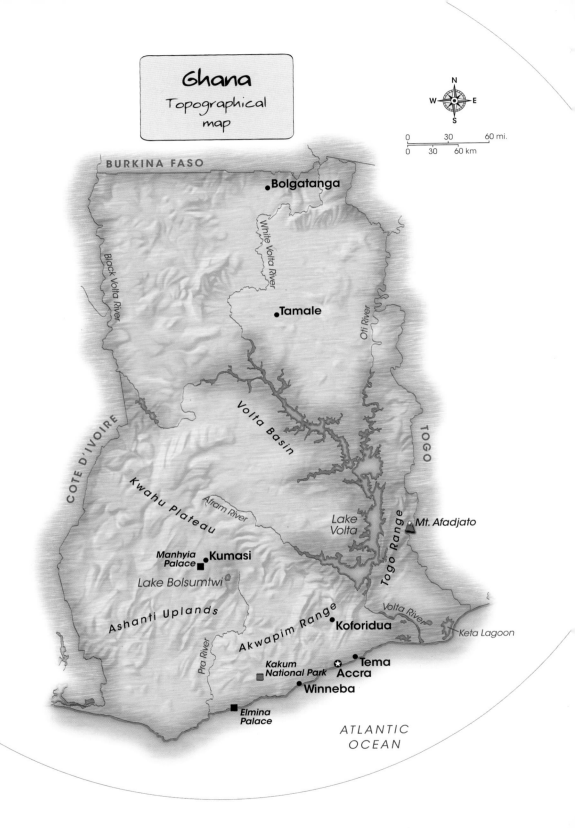

Ghana
Topographical map

BURKINA FASO

•**Bolgatanga**

Black Volta River

White Volta River

•**Tamale**

Oti River

Volta Basin

COTE D'IVOIRE

Kwahu Plateau

Afram River

Lake Volta

Togo Range

TOGO

Mt. Afadjato

Manhyia Palace ■ •**Kumasi**

Lake Bolsumtwi

Ashanti Uplands

Pra River

Akwapim Range

•**Koforidua**

Volta River

Keta Lagoon

Kakum National Park

Tema

Accra

•**Winneba**

■ Elmina Palace

ATLANTIC OCEAN

it. Highlife is played in Ghana's clubs and bars.

Hiplife is another type of modern music. Hiplife took the country by storm in the mid-1990s. It challenges highlife for airtime on local radio stations. With raps in local dialects, it appeals to the modern youth culture.

Like teens around the world, Ghanaian teens spend hours listening to music. And they have an international taste. CD collections contain albums from other African countries, the Caribbean, and the United States.

Pack Your Bags

Ghanaian teens from upper-income families often travel abroad. Ghana's Kotoka International Airport provides worldwide air service. Many Ghanaians live in other countries, and teens love visiting their kin. They also enjoy seeing how teens live in other parts of the world. However, for the majority of teens, travel is limited to their own country.

Some Ghanaian tourist attractions are also popular for school trips and family day trips. The National Museum of Ghana, for example, is an institution of national pride and heritage that many Ghanaians try to visit. Located in Accra, the museum opened on March 5, 1957, as part of Ghana's independence celebration. Exhibits range from prehistoric times to modern times and include an array of traditional musical instruments.

A Peek Inside the National Museum
The museum features:

A collection of artifacts from all over the world and from ancient Egypt, Greece, and Rome

Artifacts from African history, including domestic and military items

A collection of Ghanaian artifacts, including many Ashanti pieces, such as traditional stools and gold jewelry

A beautiful collection of fabric designs, with their history and the symbolism of the colors and shapes

An illustrated history of Ghana starting in ancient times and continuing on through contact with Europeans, the slave trade, colonialism, independence, and modern times

A contemporary section for traveling exhibitions, including an exhibit containing photographs of people around the world in everyday situations of poverty—from the United States and the United Kingdom to Asia and Africa

Elmina Castle is a popular destination for African Americans who wish to connect with their heritage.

The Slave Trade

Researchers at the University of Ghana have shed new light on how slaves were obtained. Records show that some Ghanaian tribal chiefs participated in the slave trade. They kidnapped people, then sold them into slavery. After tribal wars, prisoners taken by the winning side were sold to the traders. Records revealed that as many as 15,000 slaves were sold each year by Africans to European merchants.

In addition to museum trips, many teenagers spend vacation time exploring historical landmarks. Interesting spots include the relics of castles and forts. These stretch for hundreds of miles along Ghana's coastline.

Elmina Castle is the most famous of all the castles in Ghana. It sits astride a point at one end of a palm-fringed bay. It was built by the Portuguese in 1482 to be a thriving trade center for gold, ivory, and slaves. The castle's upper levels housed Europeans in luxury suites. The slave dungeons below were crowded and filthy. For 300 years, thousands of Africans passed through Elmina on their way to work as slaves in the Americas. Elmina Castle is one of more than 30 such strongholds built by Europeans that can be seen today. Events that shaped world history took place within its walls.

A Walk in the Treetops

A short drive from the coastal areas is Kakum National Park. Located within a rain forest, the park serves as an important conservation site. It is paradise for nature lovers. The park has one of the most varied plant and animal communities in Africa. It is home to many nearly extinct animals and plants. Elephants, monkeys, and bongo antelopes roam the forests. About 400 kinds of birds and 550 types of butterflies make their home in the rain forest. An interactive exhibit allows visitors to explore the biological connections that exist within the rain forest.

Upon entering the park, visitors experience the scents, sights, and sounds of a tropical rain forest. The guide may explain that the unusual marks on a tree are the result of an elephant's scratching its back. He may also point out a plant that serves to fight infections and heal wounds.

The most distinct feature of the park is the canopy walkway in the highest level of the forest. It offers a bird's-eye view of the forest below. The suspended, 1,148-foot (350-m) walkway has seven swinging bridges. The height and the swaying are not for the faint of heart. Despite the dizzying sensations, the walkway was built to be safe and has met world-class standards. It depends on trees and steel cables for support, although it was designed to ensure the trees' safety. From the treetops, visitors glimpse unique views of the action in the rain forest. The distant rustling of leaves can be heard as monkeys travel through the canopy.

The canopy walkway, opened in 1995, provides a unique view of the rain forest.

Looking Ahead

GHANAIAN TEENS LIVE IN A COUNTRY THAT IS STRUGGLING TO STABILIZE ITS GOVERNMENT, OVERCOME POVERTY, AND PROVIDE AN EDUCATION FOR EVERYONE. Ghana has one of the highest percentages of young people in the world. And young people are its greatest resource. The future lies with them. Today's teenagers have inherited a dual heritage. They are faced with embracing a modern way of life without giving up their traditional values. Teens represent the bridge between the old and new cultures.

Cell phones, computers, and videos are a way of life for many of today's teens. Older generations would never have dreamed of the technology teens now take for granted. Yet family ties remain important to modern-day teens. They keep in touch with their kin through festivals and celebrations. The bonds with tradition are strengthened through music, dance, and folklore.

Making Ghana a better place to live is the goal of young people in Ghana. Their desires are the same ones that spurred on their forefathers in 1957, at the time of independence. Ghana's motto, "One people, one nation, one destiny," expresses the hope of its teens.

At a Glance

Official name: Republic of Ghana

Capital: Accra

People

Population: 22,931,299

Population by age group:
0–14 years: 38.2%
15–64 years: 58.2%
65 years and over: 3.6%

Life expectancy at birth: 59.12 years

Official language: English

Other common languages: Akuapem, Akyem, Asante, Boron (Brong), Dagarte (Dagaba), Dagomba, Dangme, Ewe, Fante, Ga, Twi

Religions:
Christian: 68.8%
Muslim: 15.9%
Traditional: 8.5%
Other: 0.7%
None: 6.1%

Legal ages
Alcohol consumption: no minimum age
Driver's license: 18
Employment: 15
Marriage: 18 (females), 21 (males)
Military service: 18
Voting: 18

Government

Type of government: Constitutional democracy

Chief of state: President, elected by popular vote for four-year term

Head of government: President

Lawmaking body: Parliament, 230 seats elected by popular vote for four-year term

Administrative divisions: 10 regions

Independence: March 6, 1957 (from the United Kingdom)

National symbols: Golden Stool of the Asante, a stool dating to the 17th century that is covered in pure gold; kente cloth

National flag: Three equal horizontal colored stripes: red honors those who died in the fight for independence, gold symbolizes Ghana's mineral-rich land, and green symbolizes the country's vegetation; the black five-pointed star in the middle is the symbol of African unity in the struggle against colonialism

Geography

Total area: 95,784 square miles (239,460 square kilometers)

Climate: Tropical; warm and fairly dry along southeast coast; hot and humid in southwest; hot and dry in north; short rainy seasons vary from region to region

Highest point: Mount Afadjato, 2,904 feet (880 meters)

Lowest point: Atlantic Ocean, sea level

Major rivers: Volta, Oti, Afram, Pra

Major lake: Volta

Major landforms: Kwahu Plateau, Akwapim-Togo Ranges, Volta Basin

Economy

Currency: Ghanaian cedi

Population below poverty line: 31.4%

Major natural resources: Gold, timber, industrial diamonds, bauxite, manganese, fish, rubber, hydropower, petroleum, silver, salt, limestone

Major agricultural products: Cocoa, rice, coffee, cassava (tapioca), peanuts, corn, shea nuts, bananas, timber

Major exports: Gold, cocoa, timber, tuna, bauxite, aluminum, manganese ore, diamonds

Major imports: Machinery and transportation equipment, petroleum, chemicals, foodstuffs

Historical Timeline

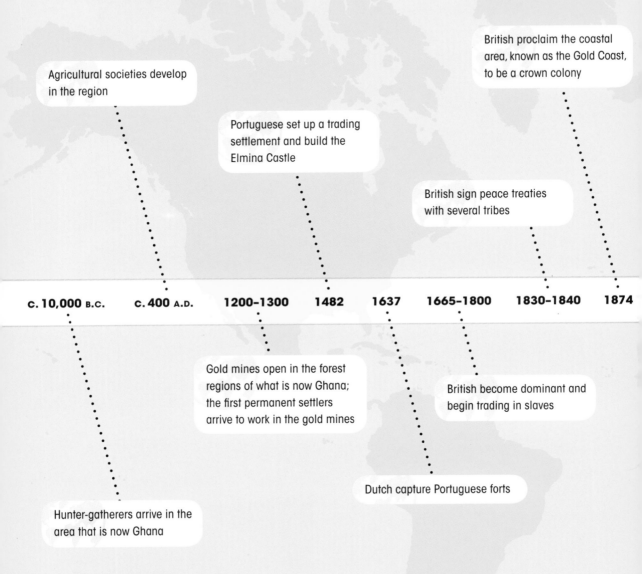

Agricultural societies develop in the region

British proclaim the coastal area, known as the Gold Coast, to be a crown colony

Portuguese set up a trading settlement and build the Elmina Castle

British sign peace treaties with several tribes

c. 10,000 B.C.   **c. 400 A.D.**   **1200–1300**   **1482**   **1637**   **1665–1800**   **1830–1840**   **1874**

Gold mines open in the forest regions of what is now Ghana; the first permanent settlers arrive to work in the gold mines

British become dominant and begin trading in slaves

Dutch capture Portuguese forts

Hunter-gatherers arrive in the area that is now Ghana

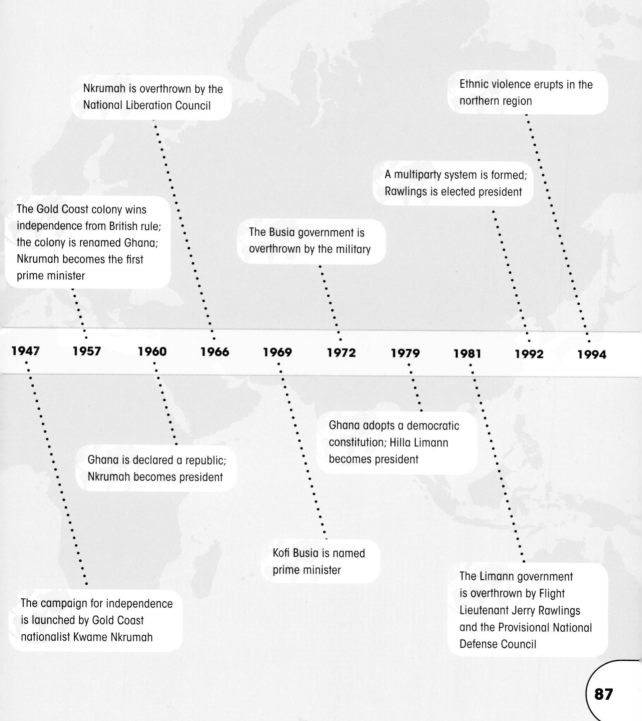

Nkrumah is overthrown by the National Liberation Council

Ethnic violence erupts in the northern region

The Gold Coast colony wins independence from British rule; the colony is renamed Ghana; Nkrumah becomes the first prime minister

A multiparty system is formed; Rawlings is elected president

The Busia government is overthrown by the military

1947   1957   1960   1966   1969   1972   1979   1981   1992   1994

Ghana adopts a democratic constitution; Hilla Limann becomes president

Ghana is declared a republic; Nkrumah becomes president

Kofi Busia is named prime minister

The Limann government is overthrown by Flight Lieutenant Jerry Rawlings and the Provisional National Defense Council

The campaign for independence is launched by Gold Coast nationalist Kwame Nkrumah

Historical Timeline

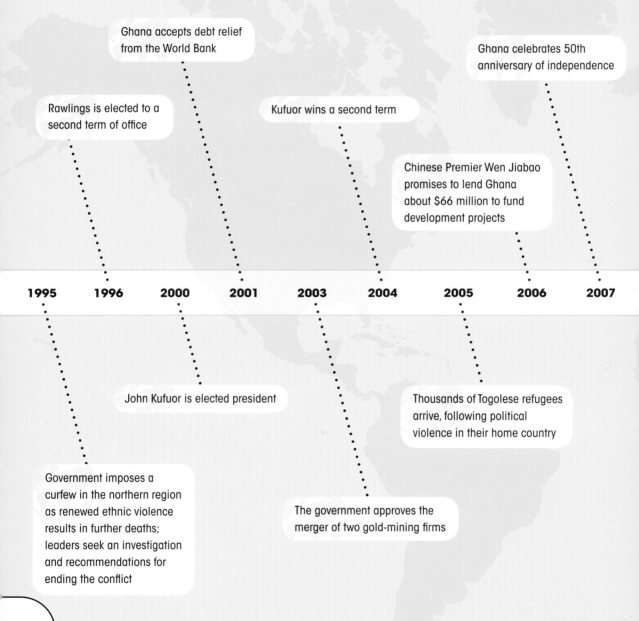

Ghana accepts debt relief from the World Bank

Ghana celebrates 50th anniversary of independence

Rawlings is elected to a second term of office

Kufuor wins a second term

Chinese Premier Wen Jiabao promises to lend Ghana about $66 million to fund development projects

1995   **1996**   **2000**   **2001**   **2003**   **2004**   **2005**   **2006**   **2007**

John Kufuor is elected president

Thousands of Togolese refugees arrive, following political violence in their home country

Government imposes a curfew in the northern region as renewed ethnic violence results in further deaths; leaders seek an investigation and recommendations for ending the conflict

The government approves the merger of two gold-mining firms

Glossary

Akan	an ethnic group of Ghana; includes the Ashanti and Fante
Ashanti	an ethnic group of Ghana; part of the larger Akan group
compound	a grouping of separate homes owned by members of the same family; often enclosed by a fence or wall
coup	a sudden change of government, often by force
customary law	laws based on traditional tribal law that was in effect before colonization
dowry	property that a woman brings to her husband in marriage
Ewe	an ethnic group of Ghana living along the eastern border
Fante	an ethnic group of Ghana; part of the larger Akan group
fertility rate	the average number of children each woman has during her lifetime
Ga	an ethnic group of Ghana living in the coastal area around Accra
Islam	a religion founded on the Arabian Peninsula in the seventh century by the Prophet Muhammad
Mole-Dagbon	an ethnic group of Ghana living in the north
Muhammad	a prophet of Islam; revelations from God to Muhammad formed the Qur'an, Islam's holy text
Muslim	a religious follower of Islam, or referring to a follower of Islam
Qur'an	the holy book of Islam, which consists mainly of the revelations Muhammad received from God during the seventh century
sub-Saharan	the part of Africa that lies south of the Sahara Desert

Additional Resources

FURTHER READING

Fiction and nonfiction titles to enhance your introduction to teens in Ghana, past and present.

Asare, Meshack. *Noma's Sand*. Legon-Accra, Ghana: Sub-Saharan Publishers, 2002.

Badoe, Adwoa. *The Pot of Wisdom: Ananse Stories*. Toronto: Douglas McIntyre; Berkeley, Calif.: Distributed in the United States by Publishers Group West, 2001.

McKissack, Patricia, and Frederick McKissack. *Life in Medieval Africa: The Royal Kingdoms of Ghana, Mali, and Songhay*. New York: Henry Holt and Company, 2005.

Montgomery, Bertha Vining, and Constance Nabwire. *Cooking the West African Way*. Minneapolis: Lerner Publications Company, 2002.

Onyefulu, Ifeoma. *Welcome Dede! An African Naming Ceremony*. London, England: Frances Lincoln; Berkeley, Calif.: Distributed in the United States by Publishers Group West, 2001.

ON THE WEB
For more information on this topic, use FactHound.
1. Go to www.facthound.com
2. Type in this book ID: 0756534178
3. Click on the Fetch It button.

Look for more Global Connections books.

Teens in Australia	*Teens in France*	*Teens in Morocco*	*Teens in Turkey*
Teens in Brazil	*Teens in India*	*Teens in Nepal*	*Teens in the U.S.A.*
Teens in Canada	*Teens in Iran*	*Teens in Nigeria*	*Teens in Venezuela*
Teens in China	*Teens in Israel*	*Teens in Russia*	*Teens in Vietnam*
Teens in Egypt	*Teens in Japan*	*Teens in Saudi Arabia*	
Teens in England	*Teens in Kenya*	*Teens in South Korea*	
Teens in Finland	*Teens in Mexico*	*Teens in Spain*	

Source Notes

Page 9, line 7: "Voices from Ghana." Oxfam's Cool Planet. 21 June 2007. www.oxfam.org.uk/coolplanet/ontheline/explore/videos/moses.htm

Page 19, column 1, line 10: "GHANA: Surging Enrollment Presents Challenges." IRIN News. 11 Oct. 2006. 21 June 2007. www.irinnews.org/Report.aspx?ReportId=61308

Page 43, column 2, line 10: "CRC 41st Session: Committee Examines Report of Ghana." United Nations Press Release. 16 Jan. 2006. 29 Nov. 2006. www.hrea.org/lists/child-rights/markup/msg00383.html

Page 56, column 2, line 16: Melissa Rick. "A Wedding and a Funeral." Ghana Semester 2006, Calvin College. 16 Dec. 2006. 12 Jan. 2007. www.calvin.edu/weblogs/ghana/a_wedding_and_a_funeral/

Page 63, column 1, line 30: "1.5 Million Children Engaged in Child Labour." GhanaHomePage. 28 Sept. 2004. 14 Dec. 2006. www.ghanaweb.com/GhanaHomePage/NewsArchive/artikel.php?ID=66792

Page 65, column 2, line 6: Eric Beauchemin. "The Exodus: The Growing Migration of Children from Ghana's Rural Areas to the Urban Centres." Catholic Action for Street Children & UNICEF. 25 March 1999. 15 Feb. 2007. www.unicef.org/evaldatabase/files/GHA_999_800_Part_1.pdf

Page 69, column 2, line 10: "Any Abuse Against Children Violates Convention on Children's Rights: Ghanaian Leader." Xinhua News Agency. 17 March 2005. HighBeam Research. 17 Dec. 2006. www.highbeam.com/doc1G1-130378024.html

Pages 84-85, "At a Glance": United States. Central Intelligence Agency. *The World Factbook—Ghana.* 19 June 2007. 20 June 2007. https://www.cia.gov/library/publications/the-world-factbook/geos/gh.html

Select Bibliography

"1.5 Million Children Engaged in Child Labour." GhanaHomePage. 28 Sept. 2004. 14 Dec. 2006. www.ghanaweb.com/GhanaHomePage/NewsArchive/artikel.php?ID=66792

"Any Abuse Against Children Violates Convention on Children's Rights: Ghanaian Leader." Xinhua News Agency. 17 March 2005. HighBeam Research. 17 Dec. 2006. www.highbeam.com/doc1G1-130378024.html

Bailey, Anne C. *African Voices of the Atlantic Slave Trade: Beyond the Silence and the Shame.* Boston: Beacon Press, 2005.

Beauchemin, Eric. "The Exodus: The Growing Migration of Children from Ghana's Rural Areas to the Urban Centres." Catholic Action for Street Children & UNICEF. 25 March 1999. 15 Feb. 2007. www.unicef.org/evaldatabase/files/GHA_999_800_Part_1.pdf

Berry, La Verle, ed. *Ghana: A Country Study.* Washington, D.C.: Library of Congress, 1995.

"CRC 41st Session: Committee Examines Report of Ghana." United Nations Press Release. 16 Jan. 2006. 29 Nov. 2006. www.hrea.org/lists/child-rights/markup/msg00383.html

Embassy of Ghana in Washington, D.C. 15 Oct. 2006. www.ghana-embassy.org/

Falola, Toyin, ed. *Teen Life in Africa.* Westport, Conn.: Greenwood Press, 2004.

Ghana. Ministry of Education, Science, and Sports. "Educational Institutions in Ghana." 13 Aug. 2007. www.edughana.net/search.htm

"GHANA: Surging Enrollment Presents Challenges." IRIN News. 11 Oct. 2006. 21 June 2007. www.irinnews.org/Report.aspx?ReportId=61308

Kuada, John, and Yao Chachah. *Ghana: Understanding the People and Their Culture*. Accra, Ghana: Woeli Publishing Services, 1999.

Kwadwo, Osel. *Asante Culture*. Kumasi, Ghana: O. Kwadwo Enterprise, 2002.

Kwadwo, Osel. *Asante History*. Kumasi, Ghana: O. Kwadwo Enterprise, 2004.

Meredith, Martin. *The Fate of Africa, from the Hopes of Freedom to the Heart of Despair: A History of 50 Years of Independence*. New York: Public Affairs, 2005.

Nkrumah, Kwame. *Africa Must Unite*. New York: International Publishers, 1972.

Omari, Peter T. *Kwame Nkrumah*. New York: Africana Publishing Corporation, 1970.

Owusu-Ansah, David. *Historical Dictionary of Ghana*. 3rd ed. Lanham, Md.: Scarecrow Press, 2005.

Rick, Melissa. "A Wedding and a Funeral." Ghana Semester 2006, Calvin College. 16 Dec. 2006. 12 Jan. 2007. www.calvin.edu/weblogs/ghana/a_wedding_and_a_funeral/

Salm, Steven J., and Toyin Falola. *Culture and Customs of Ghana*. Westport, Conn.: Greenwood Press, 2002.

Sweet, Nancy H. *Oh Africa My Africa*. Malvern, Pa.: The Marcus Horton Sweet African-American Culture Center, 1993.

Toro-Morn, Maura I., and Alicea Marixsa. *Migration and Immigration: A Global View*. Westport, Conn.: Greenwood Press, 2004.

United States. Central Intelligence Agency. *The World Factbook—Ghana*. 19 June 2007. 20 June 2007. https://www.cia.gov/library/publications/the-world-factbook/geos/gh.html

"Voices from Ghana." Oxfam's Cool Planet. 21 June 2007. www.oxfam.org.uk/coolplanet/ontheline/explore/videos/moses.htm

Wellings, Naomi. "Between Custom and Christianity." BBC News. 4 Aug. 2006. 6 June 2007. http://news.bbc.co.uk/2/hi/africa/5239902.stm

Index

About the Author
Myra Weatherly

Myra Weatherly lives in Greer, South Carolina. She is the author of more than 25 books and many articles for children, young people, and adults.

About the Content Adviser
David Owusu-Ansah, Ph.D.

David Owusu-Ansah is a professor of African studies at James Madison University in the Shenandoah Valley of Virginia. He has written scholarly articles and books on many subjects, including the history of Ghana and the Islamic culture in Africa. He is engaged in research on Islamic education in his native Ghana.